The Big6™ in Middle School:

Teaching Information and Communications Technology Skills

Barbara A. Jansen

Linworth Books

**Professional Development Resources for
K-12 Library Media and Technology Specialists**

To Larry

Library of Congress Cataloging-in-Publication Data

Jansen, Barbara A.
  The Big6 in middle schools : teaching information and communications technology skills / Barbara A. Jansen.
      p. cm.
  Includes bibliographical references and index.
  ISBN 1-58683-215-8 (pbk.)
  1. Information literacy--Study and teaching (Middle school)--United States. 2. Electronic information resource literacy--Study and teaching (Middle school)--United States. 3. Information technology--Study and teaching (Middle school)--United States. 4. Information retrieval--Study and teaching (Middle school)--United States. 5. Information literacy--Standards--United States. I. Title. II. Title: Big 6 in middle schools.
  ZA3075.J36 2007
  028.7071--dc22

                          2006025777

Published by Linworth Publishing, Inc.
3650 Olentangy River Road, Suite 250
Columbus, Ohio 43214

ISBN: 1-58683-215-8

5 4 3 2 1

Table of Contents

Table of Contents *continued*

Table of Contents continued

Table of Contents continued

Table of Contents *continued*

Table of Contents *continued*

Table of Figures

Table of Figures continued

About the Author

Barbara A. Jansen is the librarian and technology coordinator at St. Andrew's Episcopal Upper School in Austin, Texas. She also serves as part-time faculty at the University of Texas at Austin School of Information. Her latest course is "Electronic Resources for Children and Youth." She consults for the Big6 Associates with over 12 years of experience. Before becoming a librarian, she taught at Berkman Elementary in Round Rock, Texas. She has had articles published in *School Library Media Activities Monthly* and *Multimedia Schools* magazines, the *Big6 Newsletter* formerly published by Linworth Publishing and *Library Media Connection* published by Linworth. Barbara holds B.S., M.Ed., and M.L.I.S. degrees from the University of Texas at Austin. She is active in the Texas Library Association and the Texas Association of School Librarians and is a member of ALA and AASL.

Barbara is committed to collaborating with teachers to fully integrate information problem-solving, content objectives, and technology into the curriculum. In 1994, she studied the Big6 model of information problem-solving at Syracuse University with Big6™ co-authors Mike Eisenberg and Bob Berkowitz. She is a major contributor to *Teaching Information & Technology Skills: The Big6 in Elementary Schools* available through Linworth Publishing <http://www.linworth.com>. She recently published *The Principal's Guide to a Powerful Library Media Program* with Marla W. McGhee, also by Linworth. Barbara is often asked to share her ideas at conferences and professional educational training seminars for state conferences, regional service centers, and local school districts and campuses.

Acknowledgments

To my friends and colleagues, Mike Eisenberg and Bob Berkowitz, I owe much. They have generously taught me, respectfully guided me, and allowed me to participate in this wonderful process we call the Big6. Much of my professional expertise and experience is due to my close association with Mike and Bob and the Big6. Thank you for contributing Part I of this book.

Thanks to Tim McGhee, a friend and the head of our Middle School, who kindly provided me with needed documents. Also, I owe a debt of gratitude to my wonderful and creative colleagues in Round Rock I.S.D. and St. Andrew's Episcopal School for their willingness to work with me to integrate information skills into their courses of study. And, to Lucy Nazro, our Head of School and a grand champion of intellectual freedom, thanks for encouraging me to pursue challenging professional goals.

Marlene Woo-Lun, president of Linworth Publishing, and Cyndee Anderson, editor extraordinaire: Your enthusiasm and expertise are without equal. Working with you made writing this book a pleasure.

Finally, to my husband Larry: You encouraged me all the way, you cooked for me, and you spent many weekends alone while I wrote. Thanks.

Part I

by Michael B. Eisenberg and
Robert E. Berkowitz

Chapter 1

Introduction— The Need and the Solution

The Need—Living in an Information Society

It's almost a cliché to say that we live in an increasingly complex world, an information age. However, that doesn't make it any less true or any less difficult to manage. And, just as students at the middle school level are more sophisticated than those in elementary school, the nature and scope of their information problems are also more sophisticated and complicated. They too are overwhelmed by information explosion and suffer from information anxiety.

Here are some statistics that describe the information explosion that all of us face every day:

- A weekday edition of the *New York Times* has more information in it than the average 17th-century man or woman would have come across in an entire lifetime (Lewis, 1996).

- In this half-century, for the first time in history, the capacity for producing information is far greater than the human capacity to process it (Shenk, 1997).

- Regarding the estimated number of Web pages: in 1995: 1.3 million; in January 2000: more than 1 billion! (Guernsey, 2000)

Information anxiety is rampant. People even get physically sick as a result of the stress caused by information overload. It's true, and it even has its own medical term: Information Fatigue Syndrome (*Investor's Business Daily*, 1996). A study reported in the *Texas Library Journal* (Akin, 1998) noted that some of the symptoms associated with information overload are:

- Fatigue
- Stomach pains
- Failing eyesight
- Insomnia
- Forgetfulness
- Feeling overwhelmed
- Stress
- Doubt
- Vulnerability
- Anxietyousness
- Computer rage

There is simply too much information being created, stored, processed, and presented. Being overloaded is the norm; people just cannot keep up. And we aren't just talking about people in the workforce or higher education. Even elementary students are having difficulties meeting the information demands.

Dr. Melissa Gross studied the information behaviors of school-age children. Dr. Gross (1998) looked at why students were searching for information, comparing self-driven questions and needs to questions and needs imposed by others—including teachers. Not surprisingly, she found that as students progress in school, they search less and less for their own purposes. Older students search for information almost exclusively in response to imposed needs. By the time students enter high school, they spend a great deal of time reacting to information demands placed upon them by others.

Gross's findings confirm our own observations concerning the reading habits of K-12 students. In the lower grades, students have more time to read for pleasure, and take more time to read on their own. But, as they get older, students have less time for their own reading or to pursue their own interests. The demands imposed on them—the information demands—are substantial in terms of what students are asked to do as well as the difficulties of finding, processing, and presenting information.

Again, there is just too much "stuff" out there, and it is not easy to keep up. At the same time, there is an irony—yes, we are surrounded by information, but we can never seem to find what we want, when we want it, and in the form we want it.

One solution to the information problem—the one that seems to be most often adopted in schools (as well as in business and society in general)—is to speed things up. We try to pack in more and more content, to work faster to get more done. But, this is a losing proposition. It is like that old *I Love Lucy* show (Ball, 1952)—the one with Lucy and Ethel on the candy factory line. The candy comes through on the conveyor belt, and Lucy and Ethel are to wrap each piece of candy. They start out fine, feeling pretty good and saying things like, "This is easy. We can handle this." But soon the candy is moving faster and faster. They start struggling, pulling the candy off the belt, stuffing the pieces under their hats, in their mouths, and in their uniforms while exclaiming, "We're fighting a losing game!"

In education, too, speeding things up can only work for so long. Instead, we need to think about helping students to work smarter, not faster. There is an alternative to speeding things up. It is the smarter solution, one that helps students develop the skills and understandings they need to find, process, and use information effectively. This smarter solution focuses on process as well as content. Some people call this smarter solution information literacy or information skills instruction. We call it the Big6.

The Big6

The Big6 is a process model of how people of all ages solve an information problem. From practice and study, we found that successful information problem-solving encompasses six stages:

1. Task Definition
2. Information Seeking Strategies
3. Location and Access
4. Use of Information
5. Synthesis
6. Evaluation

People go through these Big6 stages—consciously or not —when they seek or apply information to solve a problem or make a decision. It is not necessary to complete these stages in a linear order, and a given stage does not have to take a lot of time. We have found that in almost all successful problem-solving situations, all stages are completed.

The Big6 and Other Approaches

The Big6 shares some similarities with other process models. For example, one generic guide to improved problem-solving and creative thinking is Koberg and Bagnall's "Problem-Solving Feedback Perspective" from *The Universal Traveler* (1980). Theirs is a seven-step approach that begins by accepting the existing situation or problem and moves to analyzing the components of the problem, defining the problem, brainstorming and selecting the solution, implementation, and evaluation. This model is characterized by its logical pattern that begins with understanding that a problem exists, and ends not with implementing a solution, but rather an evaluation of the effects of the action taken. This allows for reassessment to determine if the problem or any aspects of the problem still exist.

A process model widely used in gifted and talented education is the "Creative Problem Solving" model (Noller, Parnes, and Biondi, 1976). The five major steps in this model are:

- Fact-finding: Collect all data surrounding the problem.
- Problem-finding: Restate the problem in a more solvable form.
- Idea-finding: Brainstorm and defer judgment in an attempt to develop as many ideas as possible for solving the problem.
- Solution-finding: Select the criteria for evaluating solutions, and then apply the criteria to each possible solution. Choose the best solution.
- Acceptance-finding: Present the solution to all parties involved to decide if it would be workable. Plan, implement, and evaluate the solution.

There are also a number of information literacy process models coming from the library media field: Stripling and Pitts (1988), Kuhlthau (1985, 1993), and Pappas and Tepe (1997).

It is encouraging that there are more similarities among the models than differences (see Figure 1.1). That is, the driving force behind these models is "process." Information skills are not isolated incidents, but rather connected activities that encompass a way of thinking about and using information. Figure 1.1 compares the various information problem-solving models.

The Big6 and K-12 National Information Literacy Standards

There are also major elements of the Big6 in national standards for K-12 and for higher education. K-12 information literacy standards were developed by the American Association of School Librarians and the Association of Educational Communications and Technology (1998) as part of the *Information Power: Building Partnerships for Learning* document. The first three of the standards emphasize abilities associated with information literacy. The information literate student:

- Accesses information efficiently and effectively (Standard 1).
- Evaluates information critically and competently (Standard 2).
- Uses information accurately and creatively (Standard 3).

<http://www.ala.org/aasl/ip_implementation.html>

Figure 1.1 *Information Problem-Solving Models Comparison Chart*

Kuhlthau Information Seeking (The Big6 Skills)	Eisenberg/Berkowitz Information Problem-Solving	AASL/AECT Information Literacy Standards	Pitts/Stripling Research Process	New South Wales Information Process
1. Initiation 2. Selection	#1. Task Definition #1.1 Define the problem #1.2 Identify info requirements	1. Formulation/analysis of information need	1. Choose a broad topic 2. Get an overview of the topic 3. Narrow the topic 4. Develop thesis/purpose statement	Defining
4. Formulation (of focus)				
3. Exploration (investig. info on the general topic)	#2. Information Seeking Strategies #2.1 Determine range sources #2.2 Prioritize sources	2. Identification/appraisal of likely sources	5. Formulate questions to guide research 6. Plan for research & production	Locating
5. Collection (gather info on the focused topic)	#3. Location & Access #3.1 Locate sources #3.2 Find info	3. Tracing/locating indiv. resources 4. Examining, selecting, & rejecting indiv. resources	7. Find, analyze, evaluate resources	Selecting
	#4. Information Use #4.1 Engage (read, view, etc.) #4.2 Extract info	5. Interrogating/using individual resources 6. Recording/storing info	8. Evaluate evidence take notes/compile bib.	Organizing
6. Presentation	#5. Synthesis #5.1 Organize #5.2 Present	7. Interpretation, analysis, synth., and eval. of info. 8. Shape, presentation, and communication of info	9. Formulate questions/Organize into an outline 10. Create and present final product	Presenting
7. Assessment (of outcome/process)	#6. Evaluation #6.1 Judge the product #6.2 Judge the process	9. Evaluation of the assignment	(Reflection point—is the paper/project satisfactory)	Assessing

Standard 1, accessing information, is similar to Big6 #3 Location & Access, and Standard 3, uses information, relates to Big6 #4 Use of Information. Standard 2, evaluates information, permeates the Big6 process. That is, while it might be tempting to create a separate stage for evaluates information (coming between #4 Use of Information and #5 Synthesis, for example) we recognize that the information literate person evaluates information at every stage:

- Stage #1 Task Definition—evaluate the nature and type of information needed

- Stage #2 Use of Information Seeking Strategies—evaluate information among potential sources

- Stage #3 Location and Access—evaluate how to represent information as search terms

- Stage #4 Use of Information—evaluate what information is relevant and useful

- Stage #5 Synthesis—evaluate the specific information to apply to the task and how the information fits together

- Stage #6 Evaluation—evaluate the quality of information in the final product and effectiveness in the process.

The second set of three standards in *Information Power* relates to independent learning in terms of pursuing information related to personal interests (Standard 4), appreciation of literature and other creative expressions of information (Standard 5), and striving for excellence in information seeking and knowledge generation (Standard 6).

The last set of three standards focuses on social responsibility—contributing positively to the learning community. These standards include recognizing the importance of information to a democratic society (Standard 7), practicing ethical behavior in regard to information and information technology (Standard 8), and participating effectively in groups to pursue and generate information (Standard 9).

Higher Education

In 2000, the Association of College and Research Libraries published standards for information literacy in higher education. According to the introduction to the standards, this set of goals and outcomes was developed to encourage students to become lifelong learners <http://www.ala.org/acrl/ilintro.html>. In other words, the standards describe a student who knows how to learn and has an agile mind that will adapt quickly to the changing information landscape.

The ACRL information literacy standards are as follows:

- Standard One—The information literate student determines the nature and extent of the information needed.

- Standard Two—The information literate student accesses needed information effectively and efficiently.

- Standard Three—The information literate student evaluates information and its sources critically and incorporates selected information into his or her knowledge base and value system.

- Standard Four—The information literate student, individually or as a member of a group, uses information effectively to accomplish a specific purpose.

- Standard Five—The information literate student understands many of the economic, legal, and social issues surrounding the use of information and accesses and uses information ethically and legally.

<http://www.ala.org/ala/acrl/acrlstandards/
informationliteracycompetency. htm>

The ACRL standards focus on the student's information problem-solving process, rather than on discrete skills the student displays. Many of these standards relate to the Big6. For instance, Standard One is similar to Task Definition in that not only is the student considering what needs to be done, but also what kind of information is needed to do it. Standard Three is particularly interesting because it incorporates the idea of the learner contextualizing knowledge—adding what he finds into the framework of information he already knows.

All of these approaches to teaching information literacy skills are valid and significant. The ACRL and *Information Power* standards broach significant issues for the information age, such as ethics and citizenship, while the Big6 focuses on the information problem-solving aspect of information literacy. Obviously, we prefer and promote the Big6 to any other approach—we have found it to be a teachable process that students can relate to, and, above all, that works.

Despite its brevity compared to other processes, the Big6 is sufficient and necessary in that it encompasses the full range of the process—our research shows this. People who are natural problem solvers see themselves in the Big6 ("I've been doing this all along!"), and people who do not work as well with information find the Big6 to be a solution for many of their problems. The Big6 is widely applicable—not just for research reports and papers, but also for real-life problems such as deciding on which college to attend or how to find a summer job. Finally, the Big6 is easy to remember—it is concise, expressive, and catchy. Once students learn it, it becomes a natural part of their information toolbox.

Learning and Teaching the Big6

In addition to considering the Big6 as a process, another useful way to view the Big6 is as a set of basic, essential life skills. These skills can be applied across situations—to school, personal, and work settings. The Big6 Skills are applicable to all subject areas across the full range of grade levels. Students use the Big6 Skills whenever they need information to solve a problem, make a decision, or complete a task.

The Big6 Skills are best learned when integrated with classroom curriculum and activities. Teachers can begin to use the Big6 immediately by:

- Using the Big6 terminology when giving various tasks and assignments.
- Talking students through the process for a particular assignment.
- Asking key questions and focusing attention on specific Big6 actions to accomplish.

For example, suppose students are learning about the United States' involvement in World War II. They may start by answering a set of questions about the causes of the war or complete a worksheet or map. Later, students might take a test and also prepare a more extensive report or project. For each task that students are required to do, classroom teachers should ask, "What are you trying to accomplish? What types and how much information will you need to do it?" That's Big6 Stage #1, Task Definition.

From experience, we find that students have the most problems with Task Definition. At the same time, teachers, library media specialists, and even parents underestimate the difficulty of figuring out exactly what is to be done, the information needed to complete the task, what the result should look like once it is completed, and how the student is going to be assessed or graded.

Classroom teachers and library media specialists can use the Big6 to make an immediate impact on student performance by spending time on Task Definition whenever students get an assignment. That does not necessarily mean explaining the assignment and expectations in greater detail. Rather, it means developing techniques and lessons that help students learn to analyze an assignment, determine requirements, and get moving in the information problem-solving process.

After working on Task Definition, the teacher can then go through the rest of the Big6—prompting students to ensure that they consider the various aspects of the full process in relation to the assignment. Later, teachers or library media specialists can provide specific lessons on more Big6 stages—at the relevant time as the students work on their various assignments within a World War II unit, for example. Chapter Four provides more detail on implementation of the Big6, and the second part of this book includes examples in context.

Beyond incorporating the Big6 into everyday classroom practice, we recommend that teachers work with library media specialists and technology teachers to systematically plan to teach the Big6 Skills as part of the curriculum. Learning these essential information skills takes effort and repetition. Students need opportunities to develop in-depth expertise in each of the Big6 Skills. This requires a planned program of instruction and learning. Again, see Chapter Four for more information on implementing the Big6.

Various computer and information technology skills are integral parts of the Big6 Skills. For example, when students use word processing to write a letter, that's Big6 #5, Synthesis. When they search for information on the World Wide Web, that's Big6 #3, Location and Access. When they use e-mail to discuss an assignment with another student or the teacher, that's Big6 #1, Task Definition. Using computers can "turbo-boost" students' abilities.

Teaching and learning to use technology as part of the Big6 process is very helpful for students and teachers. Students see the connection between various technology skills and how the skills can be applied to the completion of the project. Teachers have a context for integrating technology instruction into classroom learning, assignments, and projects. Instead of focusing on the technology itself, teachers can help students think about what they want to accomplish and think how technology might help them reach their goals. The Big6-technology connection is explored in Chapter Three and also in Chapters Six through Eleven in Part II. But first, it is time to focus on the Big6 itself, to dive into the Big6 process and skills in detail.

Summary

Developing general information problem-solving skills, as well as proficiencies in specific technologies and information processes, is a major focus in education today—K-12 as well as higher education. The Big6 is a tried and tested approach to information and technology skills instruction. On the surface, the Big6 appears to be relatively simple and common sense. However, ensuring that students learn these fundamental skills for an information society takes concerted and planned effort in educational settings. Furthermore, we want our students to be more than simply aware or literate in terms of these skills; we want them to be fluent and able to demonstrate mastery across contexts.

The chapters that follow in Part I explain in more detail the Big6 model and skills; how technology is integral to Big6 use and vice versa; approaches to implementation of Big6 instruction; and finally how to assess Big6 learning. Part II provides a rich set of specific Big6 strategies and examples that can be easily adapted to a range of school and learning settings. Part III includes valuable tools to use and modify to bring the Big6 to faculties and students.

Works Cited

Akin. L. "Information Fatigue Syndrome: Malady or Marketing?" *Texas Library Journal* 74 (4).

I Love Lucy: The Classics. Dir. Asher, William. Perf. Ball, Lucille. Videocassette. 20th Century Fox, 1998.

Guernsey, L. "The Search Engine as Cyborg." *New York Times* 29 June 2000: D1.

"Information Fatigue Syndrome." *Investor's Business Daily* 1 Oct. 1996.

Koberg, D., & Bagnall. J. *The Universal Traveler: A Soft-Systems Guide to Creativity, Problem-Solving and the Process of Reaching Goals*. William Kaufman, Inc., 1980.

Kuhlthau, C. C. "Implementing a Process Approach to Information Skills: A Study Identifying Indicators of Success in Library Media Programs." *School Library Media Quarterly*, 22.1 (1993): 11-18.

Lewis, D. "Introduction to Dying for Information." 1996. [Online]. <http://about.reuters.com/rbb/research/dfiforframe.htm>.

Noller, Parnes, & Biondi. "Creative Problem Solving Model." In *Creative Behavior Workbook*. New York: Scribner, 1976.

Pappas, M. & Tepe, A. *Pathways to Knowledge: Follett's Information Skills Model Kit*. McHenry, IL: Follett Software, 1997.

Shenk, D. *Data Smog*. New York: Harper and Collins, 1997. In Kerka, S. (1997). "Information Management". *ERIC Digest*. [Online]. <http://www.ericacve.org/docs/mr00009.htm>.

Stripling, B. K., & Pitts, J. M. *Brainstorms and Blueprints: Teaching Library Research as a Thinking Process*. Englewood, CO: Libraries Unlimited, 1988.

Chapter 2

The Big6 Process and Skills

A s explained in Chapter One, the Big6 can be described both as a set of essential life skills and as a process. This is a strength of the Big6 approach—it provides a unified, process-context for learning and teaching information and technology skills.

We also find it is useful to explain the Big6 in a top-down fashion. That is, when working with students, we first try to have them understand that the Big6 is a process, from beginning to end. Then, we focus on the main six stages—from Task Definition to Evaluation. Finally, we have two sub-stages under each of the Big6. This results in 12 sub-stages, the "Little 12." The Big6 is presented in increasingly more detail below in terms of these various levels of specificity.

The Big6 is applicable to every age group and level of development—from Pre-K to senior citizen. For example, we present the idea of process and the Big6 to very young children with something called the "Super3." The three stages of the Super3 are:

- Beginning—Plan—What is my task?
- Middle—Do—What do I have to do to complete the task?
- End—Review—How will I know when I am done?

These three stages form an easy way to get young students to start thinking about how they go about solving information problems. They learn about taking "steps" in a "process." Middle school students, hopefully, will become skilled in these fundamental information problem-solving building blocks. Of course, for some students in certain situations (particularly those with learning problems), it may be desirable to start with the basics: plan—do—review.

However, as noted, the Big6 is also directly applicable in higher education and beyond. The information literacy standards identified as essential for success in higher education (developed by the Association of College and Research Libraries and endorsed by the American Association of Higher Education), closely resemble the Big6 Skills.

Levels of the Big6

Level 1: The Conceptual Level

> *Whenever students are faced with an information-based problem to solve—e.g., homework, an assignment, test, quiz, or decision—they can use the Big6 approach.*

The broadest level of the Big6 approach is the conceptual or overview level. Here, we establish the concept of process and flow. Whether we realize it or not, we undertake a process with every assignment or information task. Recognizing the process and our personal preferences for problem-solving can help us be more effective and efficient. As part of this, at this broad level, we recommend helping students learn the following:

- To recognize that most problems have a strong information component; the problems are information-rich.

- To recognize problems as such and to be able to identify the information aspects of that problem.

- To realize that information-rich problems can be solved systematically and logically.

- To understand that the Big6 Skills will help students solve the problem effectively and efficiently.

Level 2: The Big6 Skills

The second level in the Big6 approach includes the set of six distinct skills that comprise the general problem-solving method: The Big6 Skills.

When students are in a situation that requires information problem-solving, they should use these skills. We have found that completing each of these six stages successfully is necessary for solving information problems. The stages of the Big6 do not necessarily need to be completed in any particular order. Nor do students always need to be aware that they are engaging in a particular stage. However, at some point in time students must (1) define the task; (2) select, (3) locate, and (4) use appropriate information sources; (5) pull the information together; and, (6) decide that the task is complete. We do not want to leave success to chance or serendipity. We do not want students to experience frustration and task avoidance. We do want students to know the requirements and actions of each Big6 stage and the entire process so that they have a system to fall back on when they are having difficulty.

Level 3: The 12 Sub-Skills of the Big6

Through research, experience, and careful diagnosis, each of the six skills can be subdivided into two sub-skills, sometimes referred to as the "Little12." These 12 component skills provide a more specific breakdown of the overall process and allow for focused design and development of instruction.

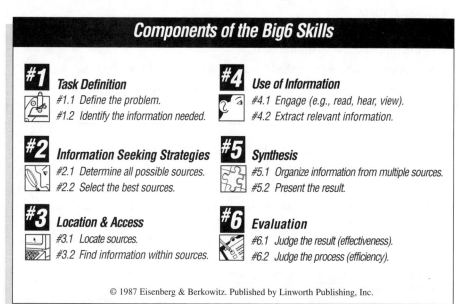

Components of the Big6 Skills

#1 Task Definition
#1.1 Define the problem.
#1.2 Identify the information needed.

#2 Information Seeking Strategies
#2.1 Determine all possible sources.
#2.2 Select the best sources.

#3 Location & Access
#3.1 Locate sources.
#3.2 Find information within sources.

#4 Use of Information
#4.1 Engage (e.g., read, hear, view).
#4.2 Extract relevant information.

#5 Synthesis
#5.1 Organize information from multiple sources.
#5.2 Present the result.

#6 Evaluation
#6.1 Judge the result (effectiveness).
#6.2 Judge the process (efficiency).

© 1987 Eisenberg & Berkowitz. Published by Linworth Publishing, Inc.

Though there is no requirement to address the Big6 components in any particular order, it is often useful to define the task before attempting to do anything else. After all, unless we know what we are expected to do, understand the nature and parameters of the problem, and can identify the information sources that will help us solve it, there is little chance for success. We would be remiss if we did not lead by example. The following sections will explain Task Definition in more detail and will provide specific examples.

#1 Task Definition

Task Definition refers to the information need or the problem to be solved. Task Definition is the ability to determine the purpose and need for information.

> **Task Definition:**
> **#1.1 Define the problem.**
> **#1.2 Identify the information needed.**

#1.1 Define the problem

What is the problem to be solved? This is the initial question that students must answer in order to solve an information problem. Defining the parameters of what is required is the key to beginning the process. How the information problem is initially defined will determine the kinds of solutions or decisions to be considered throughout the process.

Examples of Task Definition #1.1:

- Students demonstrate the ability to determine what is required in an assignment.
- Students demonstrate the ability to know what information is needed to complete the assignment.
- Students demonstrate the ability to select, narrow, or broaden topics.
- Students demonstrate the ability to formulate questions based on topics and subtopics.

#1.2 Identify the information requirements of the problem.

What information is needed in order to solve the problem or make the decision? It is necessary to diagnose the information needs before proceeding to the next skill so that maximum benefits are derived from the effort to collect information. Gathering too much information is as undesirable as gathering too little information. Once the parameters of the problem are determined, it is necessary to decide on the kinds and quantity of information that will solve the problem.

Examples of Task Definition #1.2:

- Students demonstrate the ability to pick out keywords embedded in a question or assignment.
- Students demonstrate the ability to recognize that the homework assignment requires factual information from at least three sources.
- Students demonstrate the ability to determine statements that require evidence for support.
- Students demonstrate the ability to recognize the need to gather information from people through the use of an interview, survey, or questionnaire.

Task Definition is the stage at which students determine what needs to be done and what information is needed to get the job done. We find that the number-one problem situation students can have is not knowing what is expected of them. There are a lot of reasons for this (e.g., students not paying attention, teacher not clear, task is confusing). Regardless of the reason, if students do not understand what they are to do and do not understand the basis upon which their work will be graded, they are at a tremendous disadvantage.

Teachers can help with Task Definition by bringing the task and the criteria for assessment and grading into focus. Look at your assignments. Is it clear what you are asking? Do the students truly understand? If not, you need to find ways to ensure that students do understand. Most of the time, teachers do give some form of direction concerning an assignment. We write the instructions on the board, discuss verbally what we want, or give out an assignment handout. But, communication about the task is mostly one-way and informational (making sure students have the information) rather than instructional (helping students to learn how to define tasks, zero in on critical aspects, and determine how they will fulfill the assignment at an appropriate level). Explaining an assignment is about as far as most teachers go. The assumption is that students will then know what to do and how to do it. Right? Wrong! Don't assume anything! We've found that often students in the intermediate and higher grades really do not understand what is meant by such aspects of assignments as:

- Compare and contrast
- Cite your sources
- Summarize
- Choose among
- Outline
- Describe

We must provide integrated Big6 subject-area opportunities for students to: learn effective and efficient ways to size up a task; understand what is being asked of them; and determine the nature and types of information they need to complete the task.

One way to do this is to teach Task Definition when giving students an assignment. For example, give the students the assignment and offer two or three samples of completed work for the assignment including one sample that is definitely poor, virtually a parody of the assignment. Have the students assess the samples in terms of the assignment:

- Does it do what was required?
- Is it complete?
- How could it be improved?

Another technique is to give less rather than more direction on assignments. Teachers often lead students through every step in an assignment—verbally or in writing. Sometimes it is necessary for teachers to be very directive and specific, but too often this is done without even thinking of the message being communicated. When teachers give a great deal of detail or step-by-step directions, they are doing most of the Task Definition work. They are assuming primary responsibility for Task Definition. We want students to assume ownership and responsibility. Therefore, sometimes teachers should provide less rather than more explanation.

For example, do not spell out much detail at all, or make it a game. Just give a vague, broad description of what you want the students to do on a project, homework, or even for a test. Be willing to answer any and all questions about the assignment, but put the burden on the students to find out exactly what is expected. We remind students that they need to "get inside their teachers' heads" to figure out exactly what the teacher has in mind. They need to do "brain surgery" on their teachers—without actually opening up the skull! If they don't work it out, the students will suffer the consequences.

Part of the learning process is learning how to ask good questions. When you limit the details of the assignment, you open up opportunities for your students to ask for clarification, to check for understanding, to gauge whether their approach to the problem meets your expectations. There is another benefit—one that relates to teachers and good teaching. This kind of interactive communication helps teachers to keep track of where students are having trouble or where they are finding the work too easy. They can revise the requirements as needed to adjust for errors in their underlying assumptions about what students already know. Based on problematic assumptions, teachers can go back and re-teach without throwing the assignment away. So, help your students and yourself by giving little or no direction!

The second part to Task Definition (1.2) calls for identifying the information needed and determining the information requirements of an assignment. Here, we are not talking about various sources (books, computer databases, and magazines). The sources come later. In 1.2, we want students to think about specific information needed and about how much they will need.

The type of information problem and the way students define the task will suggest to them the kinds of information they will need. This in turn will suggest to students how they can find the information. This is an exercise in "gathering" all possible sources and sorting and selecting the best sources for the task at hand. This next section will describe the Big6 stage of "Information Seeking Strategies" and offer examples of how this stage furthers the information problem-solving process.

#2 Information Seeking Strategies

Information Seeking Strategies refers to determining the alternative information sources available that are appropriate to the information need. It is a mind-expanding stage that encourages students to think broadly and creatively.

> **Information Seeking Strategies:**
> **#2.1 Determine all possible sources.**
> **#2.2 Select the best sources.**

#2.1 Determine the range of possible sources

What are all possible sources of information? Determining the universe of information sources appropriate to solving the information problem is an essential step after clarifying the task at hand. Knowledge of sources as well as imagination and creativity are important to successfully completing the step of determining likely sources.

Examples of Information Seeking Strategies #2.1:

- Students demonstrate the ability to generate a list of potential information sources, text and human, for a given information problem.
- Students demonstrate the ability to determine that an experiment is the appropriate way to gather information.
- Students demonstrate the ability to recognize various Internet capabilities (e.g., World Wide Web, e-mail, Q&A, or Ask a Librarian services) as valuable resources.
- Students demonstrate the ability to ask the library media specialist if there are any good Web sources for information.
- Students demonstrate the ability to identify electronic sources (e.g., CD-ROM, online subscription databases).

#2.2 Select the best sources

What are the best possible information sources in a particular situation and at a certain point in time? This is the key question in #2.2. It is not only important to determine the range of sources, but also it is vital to examine the sources and select those that are most likely to provide quality information to meet the task as defined.

Examples of Information Seeking Strategies #2.2:

- Students demonstrate the ability to decide that the *National Geographic* CD-ROM is the perfect source to complete the homework assignment.
- Students demonstrate the ability to decide that a segment from a current Public Broadcasting Service program is a better source of information about whales than a magazine article from 10 years ago.

- Students demonstrate the ability to assess the value of free Web sites in relation to their task.
- Students demonstrate the ability to select sources that are suitable to meet the information need (e.g., current, authoritative, accurate, understandable, useful, available).

Once students understand the task or problem and have some idea about the types of information needed, their attention must turn to the range of possible information sources. This is the stage when students examine the possible information sources, and then select the sources that are most appropriate and available. Once they get into it, students are generally quite good at brainstorming sources. The goal is to get them to think broadly.

For example, when starting a report or project, students tend to rely on the usual sources—the Internet, books, reference materials, and magazines. There are other sources that they generally overlook. These neglected sources include subscription databases, local and regional topic experts, historical societies, and documentary films. Students might greatly enhance their projects by consulting these sources. Students must first think broadly about all types of sources. They must then narrow and select those sources that really meet their needs in terms of richness of information and availability. Brainstorm and narrow—these are critical thinking skills that can be developed with students of all ages.

Teachers can build various brainstorming activities into their classroom to help students identify the wide range of possible sources. For example, break the students into small groups and have each group brainstorm and narrow related to a topic, then compare results with the whole class. Or, present an assignment and a list of possible sources. Then, on a card, have students write down their source of choice and their reason for selecting that source.

Identifying the range of all possible sources and even selecting the best sources can be fun, but it is not very helpful for solving a problem unless the students are able to actually retrieve the information they need. The Big6 recognizes this dilemma by requiring that students have the skills to locate and access information. That is the next stage of the Big6.

#3 Location & Access

Location and Access refers to finding and retrieving information sources as well as specific information within sources.

> **Location & Access:**
> **#3.1 Locate sources.**
> **#3.2 Find information within sources.**

#3.1 Locate sources

This is the stage where students find the sources physically or electronically. They need to determine where the sources are located—in the classroom, library, or online. How are the sources organized in those places— alphabetically by topic or author, by the Dewey Decimal Classification System, not at all? Are there electronic tools for access such as an online catalog or is the information itself available on the Web or some other electronic format? And, if the source is a person, can she be reached by telephone or e-mail, or is it best (or necessary) to meet her in person?

Examples of Location & Access #3.1:

- Students demonstrate the ability to locate sources in the library.
- Students demonstrate the ability to search subscription databases.
- Students demonstrate the ability to find sources by Dewey Decimal number.
- Students demonstrate the ability to find resources throughout their community.
- Students demonstrate the ability to arrange to interview a key civic leader.

#3.2 Find information within sources

This stage refers to actually getting to the information in a given source. Once the source is located, students must find the specific information they need. This is not the most glamorous of skills, but it is essential nevertheless. And, there is a key to this stage—it is learning to search for and then use . . . the INDEX! This is the library media specialist's secret weapon. Library media specialists and teachers have traditionally taught students about indexes, but doing so within the Big6 process makes a lot more sense to children.

Examples of Location & Access #3.2:

- Students demonstrate the ability to use the index in their textbook.
- Students demonstrate the ability to use a table of contents.
- Students demonstrate the ability to look up locations on a map.
- Students use a search tool in an electronic encyclopedia to get to the needed section.
- Students demonstrate the ability to skim to find the appropriate material on a Web site.
- Students use various finding tools on a Web site.

Location and Access should be the easiest stage, but it often is not. It is also not a very exciting or particularly interesting stage. But, it does need to be completed if your children are to succeed. The goal in this stage is to locate the sources selected under the Information Seeking Strategies stage, and then actually to get to the information in those sources. In the past, library media specialists and teachers spent a great deal of time on this part of the process. That's changing because they realize that Location and Access is only part of the overall process.

Again, a crucial tool that can save a lot of time in Location and Access of sources is an index. Indexes of various kinds (yellow pages, directories in shopping malls, back-of-the-book indexes, online magazine databases) make it easier to find information. Indexes may not be exciting, but they really do save time and effort. Students should always be on the lookout for indexes and they should know how to use them. Of course, indexes are not the only way to locate and access information. Sometimes we just browse through the shelves, skim a book, or surf the Internet!

Teachers can help their students with Location and Access in many ways. For example, they can help in math by teaching how to search the textbook or class notes for examples of how to solve a type of problem. Or, they can demonstrate by using a back-of-the-book index while the children watch. Just recognizing "indexes" is a valuable lesson. Have students keep a log for one week of every time they used an index—what, why, how, and how useful was it?

Once students find the information, they need to know that it is appropriate to the task, and they need to be able to use it effectively. This aspect of completing a project can frustrate students' ultimate success because they have their own set of assumptions (e.g., about expectations, usefulness of information, clarity of instruction) that get in the way of effectively using the materials they found. The Big6 tackles this aspect of student learning by focusing them on engaging the information and extracting what is really relevant. That's the next stage—#4, Use of Information.

#4 Use of Information

Use of Information refers to the application of information to meet defined information tasks.

> **Use of Information:**
> **#4.1 Engage (e.g., read, hear, view).**
> **#4.2 Extract relevant information.**

#4.1 Engage (e.g., read, hear, view) the information in a source

What information does the source provide? Ultimately, to gain useful and meaningful information from a source requires students to read, listen, or view in some form. We call these actions "engaging" the information and it is crucially important. The widespread emphasis on reading and its role in overall achievement attests to the importance of this stage.

Examples of Use of Information #4.1:

- Students demonstrate the ability to listen and comprehend.
- Students demonstrate the ability to watch an instructional video and recognize relevant information.

- Students demonstrate the ability to conduct an interview—in person or via e-mail.
- Students demonstrate the ability to read and understand various forms of graphs.
- Students demonstrate the ability to interact with a Web site.

#4.2 Extract information from a source

What specific information is worth applying to the task? This is establishing "relevance" and can only be determined when students read, listen, or watch effectively. Even when students do locate sources and find appropriate information, they must be able to read and understand, or listen effectively, or watch for key concepts and examples relevant to their task. Otherwise, the source will not help them meet their information need. Extraction also involves taking the information with you in some way. This can include note taking, copying and pasting, downloading, filming or recording, or sometimes just remembering.

Examples of Use of Information #4.2:

- Students demonstrate the ability to list the key points in an article, chapter, or Web site related to a specific question or topic.
- Students demonstrate the ability to underline or highlight the topic statement from a magazine article on the technological revolution.
- Students demonstrate the ability to summarize concisely.
- Students demonstrate the ability to copy and paste information from a Web page or electronic resource—and to correctly cite the source.
- Students demonstrate the ability to download clip art.
- Students demonstrate the ability to properly cite information from any type of information source.

The previous Big6 stage, Location and Access, is easy compared to actually making use of the information found in the sources. This requires students to: read, view, or listen; decide what is important for the particular task at hand; and finally to extract the needed information. This is not always easy to do, and can be quite time-consuming.

Classroom teachers and library media specialists already do a great deal to develop Use of Information skills. For example, lessons and exercises on reading, viewing, or listening for a purpose, comprehension, and note taking all help students to develop their ability to recognize and extract relevant information. What's sometimes missing is context, i.e., helping students to make the connection between these Use of Information actions and their place within the overall information problem-solving process.

Teachers and library media specialists can also focus various ways to skim or scan—in print or electronically—and then show students how to "capture" that information for use in their own work. The Web, subscription databases, digital and video cameras, cassette recorders, and other technological tools provide new ways for students to capture and use information. Of course, there is greater potential than ever before for the misrepresentation of work as their own. Therefore, another key component of Use of Information is to help students learn that properly crediting authors and sources from all types of formats is essential. We can also help students learn efficient ways to properly cite and credit.

Putting a project together or completing an assignment is a lot like baking a cake. Once all the separate ingredients are identified, extraneous items put aside, and the relevant ingredients ordered and handled correctly, they need to be combined. Synthesis is the fifth stage of the Big6. This is the point when students pull together the information and begin to create the final project. Today, we have powerful new technology tools for Synthesis—from word processing to desktop publishing to multimedia and Web authoring. Therefore, Synthesis includes instruction on using these tools while at the same time going beyond the glitz to focus on developing good techniques and skills for organizing and presenting information in writing, graphic, and oral forms.

#5 Synthesis

Synthesis refers to the integration and presentation of information from a variety of sources to meet the information need as defined.

> **Synthesis:**
> **#5.1 Organize information from multiple sources.**
> **#5.2 Present the result.**

#5.1 Organize information from multiple sources

The key question in Synthesis is: "How does the information from all of the sources fit together?" This skill focuses on determining the best ways to pull together, integrate, and organize the information to meet the task.

Examples of Synthesis #5.1:

- Students demonstrate the ability to create chronological timelines and charts relating key dates and events.
- Students demonstrate the ability to organize different pieces of information in different formats into a logical whole.
- Students demonstrate the ability to use word processing to revise the sequence, flow, or outline of content in a paper, report, or project.
- Students demonstrate the ability to combine information from a range of print and electronic sources and from their own notes.
- Students demonstrate the ability to arrange and rearrange information using PowerPoint or other multimedia presentation software to arrange information.

- Students demonstrate the ability to properly cite Web or other electronic sources in context and in bibliographies.
- Students demonstrate the ability to represent a still life in different media.
- Students demonstrate the ability to create and label maps or other representations of geographic information.
- Students demonstrate the ability to graph data collected during a science experiment using electronic spreadsheets or other tools.

Synthesis involves organizing and presenting the information—putting it all together to complete a defined task. Sometimes Synthesis can be as simple as relaying a specific fact (as in answering a short-answer question) or making a decision (deciding on a topic for a report, a product to buy, an activity to join). At other times, Synthesis can be very complex and can involve the use of several sources, a variety of media or presentation formats, and the effective communication of abstract ideas.

Computer applications can help students organize and present information. Word processing, graphics programs, desktop publishing, databases, spreadsheets, Web authoring, and presentation packages can all help students put information together and present it effectively. Teachers do not have to be experts with any of these tools in order to help students learn to use them effectively. Teachers can arrange for library media specialists, technology teachers, or even expert students to help students learn the capabilities and features of a program. But, the important aspects are still the same regardless of tool or format:

- Using information to draw conclusions.
- Forming judgments based on evidence.
- Creating a logical argument.
- Organizing and communicating in a way that makes sense.
- Drawing conclusions.
- Presenting a coherent whole.

Throughout the information problem-solving process, students should reflect on where they are and how they are doing. Students need to figure out where they are in the project or assignment, whether they are making progress toward its completion, how good it is, and how well they are using the available time. This is Evaluation, Big6 stage 6. But Evaluation is not meant to just be the final action that students take—a summary at the end. Evaluation is an activity that students need to get in the habit of doing all the time.

#6 Evaluation

In the Big6, evaluation refers to judgments on two different matters: (1) the degree to which the information problem is solved, and (2) the information problem-solving process itself.

> **Evaluation:**
> **#6.1 Judge the result (effectiveness).**
> **#6.2 Judge the process (efficiency).**

#6.1 Judge the result

Is the task completed; is the problem resolved? This is the primary concern in Evaluation. While working on an assignment, students should routinely monitor their own progress. Sometimes, they might realize that they do not quite understand the task, and that they need to go back and change or adjust the task. Students must also be able to recognize that they are finished and that the quality of the result is at the level they (and their teacher) desire. One important way that students can accomplish this "summative evaluation" is to be able to compare their resulting product, paper, or report (or other form of assignment) in relation to clearly understood criteria.

Examples of Evaluation #6.1:

- Students demonstrate the ability to evaluate multimedia presentations for both content and format.
- Students demonstrate the ability to determine whether they are on the right track in science labs and experiments.
- Students demonstrate the ability to judge the effectiveness of three different forms of information products (e.g., subscription database, Web site, book).
- Students demonstrate the ability to rate their projects based on a set of criteria that they set themselves.

6.2 Judge the information problem-solving process

For students to continue to improve their information problem-solving abilities, they need to learn how to assess their actions. They should also consider how they can be more efficient—in terms of saving time and effort—in carrying out each component skill.

- Students demonstrate the ability to set criteria for quality reports.
- Students demonstrate the ability to assess their confidence in taking practice tests.
- Students demonstrate the ability to thoughtfully consider how well they were able to use electronic sources throughout their project.
- Students demonstrate the ability to compare the amount of time that they estimate should be spent on an assignment with the actual amount of time spent.
- Students demonstrate the ability to reflect on their level of personal effort and time spent during their work on the assignment.

In the Evaluation stage, students should reflect on the process and result of their work. Are they pleased with what they are doing or have completed? If they could do the project again, what might they do differently? Evaluation determines the effectiveness and efficiency of the information problem-solving process. Effectiveness is another way of saying, how good is the product? What grade are you likely to get? Efficiency refers to time and effort. If the children were to do the work again, how could they do as well, but save some time and effort?

It is important to get students to reflect on their performance. They need to think about their result and decide if they are pleased with it. It is not always necessary to get a top grade; sometimes "okay" is enough. At other times, they should want to strive for excellence. Students need to understand and recognize the difference. They also need to think about the process. Where did they get stuck? Where did they waste time? All this is so they can make changes next time. These kinds of self-reflection actions are true learning experiences. When students are self-aware, they evaluate themselves and can change their behavior for the better in the future.

There are a number of strategies that teachers can use to focus students' attention on Evaluation. For example, provide "time-out" reflection points during the process to assess how well they are doing, if they are clear about the assignment, and where in the process they are having difficulties. Have students keep a log during an assignment and later discuss steps taken, successes, and areas for improvement. When completing major assignments, ask students to include a one-page "process review" piece in which they discuss their activities, successes and concerns, and how they might improve in the future.

Teachers can also provide clear directions and criteria for assessment. This does not mean being over-detailed or laborious. It means making sure that students understand what they are being asked to do and how they will be graded.

Scoring guides or rubrics are another way to help students assess themselves or fully understand how they will be assessed. Ultimately, evaluation should encourage students to improve and help them to do so. Classroom teachers and teacher-librarians can work with students on identifying the most difficult aspect of an assignment and what students might do differently next time.

Evaluation activities are not just for the end of the process. Teachers can coach students to reflect during each stage of the information problem-solving process. In designing instruction, plan for frequent opportunities to check for understanding and progress. Also, be available to help trouble-shoot when problems arise. These are not just content or subject comprehension problems, but problems in relation to the process, in terms of what to do next or how to proceed.

And finally, to reinforce an earlier point, a goal in middle schools is to reinforce students' abilities to assess themselves. Students' self-assessments should be similar to those of their teachers. One technique is to have students estimate their grades before handing in an assignment. Also ask, "if you had more time, what would you do differently and why?" The students do not have to go back and actually make the changes; just recognizing how they would do something differently reflects substantive learning.

In Evaluation, we want to encourage students to gauge their own growth, progress, strengths, and skills in a way that is useful to their continued learning. Evaluation is the culmination of the entire process, but it is often the part of the process that receives the least attention. Teachers and library media specialists should carefully consider activities and exercises to emphasize Evaluation. In doing so, they actually help students in every stage of the Big6 Skills.

Summary

This chapter offered an extensive view of the Big6 process and the specifics of the Big6 Skills. The next chapter directly addresses the issue of technology. Considering technology and technology tools within the Big6 process provides students with a powerful context for becoming effective and efficient users of information.

Chapter 3

Technology with
a Big6 Face

Introduction

"Students must be proficient in using computer technology."

This is a clear goal in K-12 education today, and schools worldwide are scrambling to improve the level of computer technology in schools as well as to infuse computer technology into the instructional program. These efforts are impressive in terms of the numbers of computers, the installation of networks, and the level and speed of Internet connectivity.

It is also encouraging to note a growing realization that being computer literate is more than simply being able to operate a computer. First, there is recognition that it's not just computers that we want students to be able to use. We want them to be literate in using the full range of information technologies—productivity tools, communications capabilities, information resources and systems, hand-held devices, and more. Second, the focus is shifting from "teaching computing in a separate class located in a computer lab" to "students learning to use the full range of information technology for a purpose as part of the subject area curriculum."

We want students to know more than a particular set of commands or even how to use a particular type of software. We want students to use technology flexibly and creatively. We want them to be able to size up a task, recognize how technology might help them to fulfill the task, and then use the technology to do so.

Helping students learn to apply technology in these ways requires a change in the way computer skills are traditionally taught in school. It means moving from teaching isolated "computer skills" to teaching integrated "information and technology skills." Integration means infusing technology in the curriculum, but equally important, it means infusing technology into each stage of the Big6 information problem-solving process. The Big6 provides the framework for learning and applying technology. Individual information and technology skills take on new meaning when they are integrated within the Big6, and students develop true "computer literacy" because they have genuinely applied various computer and technology skills as part of the learning process.

Moving from teaching isolated computer skills to helping students learn integrated information and technology skills is not just a good idea. It's essential if we are to put students in a position to succeed in an increasingly complex and changing world. Peter Drucker, well-known management guru, stated that "executives have become computer-literate... but not many executives are information literate" (Drucker A16). In our view, Drucker is saying that being able to use computers is not enough. Executives must be able to apply computer skills to real situations and needs. Executives must be able to identify information problems and be able to locate, use, synthesize, and evaluate information in relation to those problems. These are the same skill needs that exist for all people living in an information society.

There are many good reasons for moving from teaching isolated computer skills to teaching integrated information and technology skills. Technology is changing at a breathtaking pace and will continue to do so for the foreseeable future. In a speech at the 1997 National Educational Computing Conference in Seattle, Bill Gates stated that computing power has increased one million times over the past 20 years and will likely do so again in the next 20 years.

A million times more powerful! Will learning isolated specific skills such as keyboarding, word processing, or even World Wide Web searching suffice? Clearly not. Will learning to use whatever technologies come along to boost our abilities within the overall information problem-solving process suffice? Absolutely. That is what it means to look at technology from a Big6 perspective, to give technology a Big6 face.

Technology and the Big6

It's actually relatively easy to view technology from a Big6 perspective. Let's take a typical basic technology: a pencil and paper. In Big6 terms, how can a pencil and paper help us be more productive? Clearly, a pencil and paper boost our ability to synthesize, organize, and present information (Big6 #5).

What are the electronic equivalents of a pencil and paper, the tools that help us even more to synthesize? There are word processing and desktop publishing, HyperStudio, PowerPoint, and other presentation software programs. All these are used to organize and present information (Big6 #5).

Here is another basic technology: a phone book. The phone book is an aid for Big6 #3—Location and Access. What are the electronic technology equivalents to the phone book? There are the online subscription databases, Web browsers and search engines (e.g., Yahoo, Lycos, Google).

Other technologies can be viewed in this way. Similar to books, full-text databases, CD-ROM encyclopedias, and other digital resources are part of an effective Information Seeking Strategy (Big6 #2) and are read/viewed/listened to for information (Big6 #4). When a face-to-face meeting is not possible, e-mail is highly useful for linking students with their teachers or with other students for Task Definition activities (Big6 #1), and later for Evaluation (Big6 #6). And more and more, students are learning to take notes and extract information by using the copy and paste functions in word processing software.

When integrated into the information problem-solving process, these technological capabilities become powerful information tools for students. Figure 3.1 provides a summary of how some of today's technologies fit within the Big6 process.

Figure 3.1: Computer Capabilities and the Big6™

Word processing	SYNTHESIS (writing) USE OF INFORMATION (note taking)
Spell/grammar checking	EVALUATION
Desktop publishing	SYNTHESIS
Presentation/Multimedia software	SYNTHESIS
Electronic spreadsheets	SYNTHESIS
Online library catalog	LOCATION & ACCESS
Electronic magazine index	LOCATION & ACCESS USE OF INFORMATION
Full-text electronic databases	INFORMATION SEEKING STRATEGIES USE OF INFORMATION
Brainstorming software	TASK DEFINITION
Copy-paste (in various programs)	USE OF INFORMATION

Examples of Technology in Big6 Contexts

Integrating technology instruction with the Big6 provides a context for technology skills instruction. It also helps students learn to apply technology flexibly and creatively.

In Chapter Four, we explain the importance of two contexts—the Big6 process and the subject area classroom curriculum—to effective Big6 Skills instruction. This is particularly true for teaching technology skills. We avoid teaching technology skills in isolation when we combine them with the Big6 process and with real subject area curriculum and assignments.

For example, a seventh grade class is studying regions of the state and comparing various features (e.g., geography, population, industry, and special attributes). The assignment is to create a comparative chart that highlights differences and similarities.

As students go through the work for the assignment, they engage in various stages of the Big6. The teacher recognizes that this might be a good opportunity to teach technology and the Big6. She arranges with the library media specialist for the students to learn about searching for books in various digital resources (Big6 #3, Location and Access). The students will also search on the World Wide Web and compare what they found in terms of quality, amount of information, and time and effort.

The teacher also speaks to the technology teacher about possible programs to help the students create charts (Big6 #5, Synthesis). The technology teacher recommends a draw/paint program and schedules the class for a special lesson.

This is a powerful example of the integration of technology, the Big6, and curriculum. Students are learning to use technology as part of the information problem-solving process to perform better in classroom curriculum.

An English language arts class is studying an award-winning historical novel. Working in groups, the students are to create a formal report on the historical context of the novel that they selected. The students brainstorm possible sources and one group decides that talking to someone who is an expert in history and American literature is a good idea; perhaps this person is teaching at a university (Big6 #2, Information Seeking Strategies). However, they realize they have no way of getting to a university or anywhere else by themselves (Big6 #3, Location and Access). Their teacher suggests they send an e-mail to the library media specialist asking what to do. They do so and she suggests conducting the interview through the Internet, either by e-mail or chat.

But, where can they find a likely university and the e-mail address of someone there who teaches this subject (Big6 #3, Location and Access)? The students realize they can use a Web search engine to locate the Web sites of various universities, which probably include lists of staff.

Over the next few days, the students make contact with a university professor who agrees to answer their questions via e-mail. The students e-mail the questions and are excited when they get a response in three days. They copy and paste from the e-mail into a word processing document and note the name of their contact, e-mail address, and dates of the e-mail exchanges.

Technologies incorporated in this example include the use of a messaging or e-mail program, Web search engine, Web browser, and word processing program. The copy-paste function from e-mail is also an important skill for the students to learn. Another twist to this assignment would be to use multimedia presentation software to create and present the report instead of the traditional written format (Big6 #5, Synthesis).

When we reflect on integrating technology skills into teaching and learning, we realize that it is not necessary to change the fundamentals of quality instruction or the information problem-solving perspective that is at the heart of the Big6 Skills approach. The implementation of technology through the Big6 works in the following ways:

- Develops students' problem-solving, complex thinking, and information management abilities.

- Enables students to become comfortable with technology and understand that the technologies are valuable tools to help them perform their work.

- Focuses students' attention on using technologies as tools to extend knowledge and to individualize learning.

- Develops an active participatory learning process in which students become self-directed learners.

- Facilitates integrating technology across all grades and into all disciplines.

- Assists teachers to change their roles from presenters of information to "learning coaches" who offer tools and advice.

- Helps teachers introduce technology and have students use technologies even if the teachers are not experts themselves.

Implementing technology within the Big6 process is easy, direct, and powerful. It also encourages classroom teachers, library media specialists, and technology teachers to collaboratively design instruction that can intentionally create challenging and exciting learning experiences. Such opportunities expand the scope of new technology use by all students.

The Big6 and the Internet

The Internet provides an overwhelming set of technologies that deserve special note. The World Wide Web, in particular, provides unprecedented access to information, along with some serious challenges. For the first time in history, we have immediate access to massive amounts of information. The sheer volume is mind-boggling. One study by NEC Research Institute and Inktomi Corporation estimates that the Web had 320 million pages in

December 1997, 820 million pages by February 1999, and more than 1 billion in February of 2000. Compare this to 18 million published works in the Library of Congress (Glanz, 2000).

At the same time, we constantly hear that yes, there is a lot of information on the Web, but still it's hard to find what you want. How do you make sense of it all? How do you really use it effectively and efficiently?

Again, we fall back on the Big6 process. To make sense of the Web involves most of the Big6 process—from Task Definition to Evaluation. Figure 3.2 shows how Internet and Web capabilities fit within the Big6 context. All stages of the Big6 can benefit from use of the Internet and Web.

Figure 3.2: Internet Capabilities and the Big6

E-mail, chat, messaging (ICQ)	TASK DEFINITION INFORMATION SEEKING STRATEGIES LOCATION & ACCESS USE OF INFORMATION SYNTHESIS EVALUATION
Mailing lists (listservs), newsgroups, chat, wikis	TASK DEFINITION INFORMATION SEEKING STRATEGIES LOCATION & ACCESS USE OF INFORMATION SYNTHESIS EVALUATION
Web browsers (Netscape, Firefox, Internet Explorer)	INFORMATION SEEKING STRATEGIES LOCATION & ACCESS
Search engines (Google, Yahoo!), etc.	INFORMATION SEEKING STRATEGIES LOCATION & ACCESS
Portals (My Yahoo!, MSN, AOL)	INFORMATION SEEKING STRATEGIES LOCATION & ACCESS USE OF INFORMATION
Web authoring (HTML)	SYNTHESIS
Web sites, RSS	USE OF INFORMATION

Here are some Big6 suggestions for using the Web in teaching:

Task Definition: Don't start with the Web; start with the problem. Discuss what the students are trying to accomplish and what the result might look like.

Information Seeking Strategies: Consider options and alternatives, even within the Web. Big6 #2.1 involves determining possibilities, #2.2 is to choose the best sources given the situation. That means applying criteria, such as closeness to the problem, accuracy, currency, and authority of each Web site. Students should be able to explain why they chose to use a particular Web site based on one or more of these criteria.

Location and Access: Search tools are a key! Discuss how the various search systems differ. Students should be able to explain why they prefer one over another.

Use of Information: This stage involves selecting good information, again based on applying criteria. Discuss criteria and how to make choices based on criteria.

Synthesis: Ease-of-use is the primary concern in Synthesis. How easy is it to find information on a Web site? Is it logical, easy to understand, simple to navigate?

Evaluation: One aspect to focus on is efficiency, saving time and effort while maintaining quality. This relates directly to the original concern of not being overwhelmed by information. What are some strategies for using the Web for a purpose, but doing so without wasting considerable time?

We cannot overemphasize that the key for classroom, library, and technology teachers is not to focus on the Web or technology itself. We should focus on the learning goals, the content, and the Big6 process, and then make the technology connection. For example, helping students become discriminating users of information—applying good judgment in selecting sources and information within sources—is central to the Big6 stages of Information Seeking Strategies and Use of Information. These essentials are transferable, long-term Big6 abilities. The way to help students gain these abilities is through integrating subject-area Big6-technology instruction.

Summary

This chapter provided a conceptual framework and approach for helping students learn and use technology in meaningful ways. Technologies can boost students' abilities to solve curriculum-based information problems. The key is to use technology within the Big6 process. Figure 3.3 presents the Big6 view and how various current technologies fit into the Big6.

The next chapter turns to the question of implementation. Teaching the Big6 and Web skills in context means determining when students actually are working on a project or assignment that lends itself to using the Web. Also, it's not necessary to cover all Big6 Skills in each context. For example, with one assignment, we might teach the Web and Task Definition; in a later unit we would emphasize Information Seeking Strategies or Evaluation. The key is to make the connection, to link students' learning about the Web into a relevant Big6 and curricular context.

When it comes to technology, we can't know it all or even anticipate what it might be. Remember the earlier quote from Bill Gates: in 20 years we will have computers that are a million times more powerful than those of today. No one really knows into what forms this capability will translate.

What we as educators can do is to ask the key questions with the Big6 in mind:

- What do we want to accomplish from a content and a Big6 perspective?
- How can the technology help to do it?
- In our schools, classrooms, libraries, labs, and homes—what will it take to use the technology in this way?
- Will this use really make a difference for students in terms of effectiveness and efficiency?
- Is it worth taking the time and effort to integrate the technology instruction now?
- If yes, what will it take? How can we provide meaningful learning opportunities that integrate content, process, and technology?

Works Cited

Drucker, P. "Be Data Literate—Know What to Know." *Wall Street Journal* 1 Dec. 1992: A16.

Glanz, W. "Information Overload Weighs Down Web." *Insight on the News* 28 Feb 2000, 16.8: 27.

Figure 3.3 The Big6 and Technology

TASK DEFINITION	E-mail, group discussions (mailing lists, newsgroups), brainstorming software, chat (IRC, MOO, Palace), videoconferencing (CUSeeMe), groupware, wikis
INFO SEEKING STRATEGIES	Online catalogs, info retrieval, electronic resources (CD-ROMs, intranet), WWW/net resources, AskERIC[1], Internet Public Library[2], online discussion groups (mailing lists), wikis
LOCATION & ACCESS	Online catalogs, electronic indexes, WWW browsers (Netscape[3], Internet Explorer), search engines (Yahoo[4], Alta Vista[5], Lycos[6], Hotbot[7]), AskERIC, AskA+ Locator[8], telnet, ftp, e-mail, wikis, RSS
USE OF INFORMATION	Upload/download, word processing, copy-paste, outliners, spread-sheets, databases (for analysis of data), statistical packages, wikis, RSS
SYNTHESIS	Word processing, desktop publishing, graphics, spreadsheets, database management, hypermedia, presentation software, down/up load, ftp, e-journals, mailing lists, newsgroups, Web/HTML authoring, wikis
EVALUATION	Spell/grammar checkers, e-mail, online discussions (listservs, newsgroups), chat (IRC, MOO, Palace), videoconferencing (CUSeeMe), groupware, wikis

[1]AskERIC—http://www.askeric.org

[2]Internet Public Library—http://www.ipl.org/

[3]Netscape—http://www.netscape.com/

[4]Yahoo—http://www.yahoo.com/

[5]AltaVista—www.altavista.com

[6]Lycos—http://www.lycos.com/

[7]Hotbot—http://hotbot.lycos.com/

[7]AskA+ Locator—http://www.vrd.org/locator/index.html

The BIG 6

Chapter 4

Implementing the Big6: Context, Context, Context

> **Warning: Teaching Information & Technology Skills Out of Context is Hazardous to Your Students' Health.**

Introduction: Contexts

In real estate, they talk about the three key elements: location, location, and location. We look at the key elements to implementing a meaningful Big6 information and technology skills program in a similar way: context, context, and context.

There are actually two essential contexts for successful Big6 Skills instruction: (1) the process itself and (2) real needs—either curricular or personal. When we talk about an integrated Big6 Skills program, we mean integrating Big6 learning and teaching in both of these contexts.

Another way to think of these contexts is as "anchors." When students are engaged in a task or solving a problem, it is easy to get lost. But, they are in a much better position to succeed if, at any point in time, they can identify the two anchors:

#1-Where are they in the Big6 process?
#2-What is the curriculum or personal need?

Let us look at each of these contexts in more detail.

Context 1: The Big6 Process

As explained in Chapter Two, the Big6 is a process composed of six stages of skills. While successful information problem-solving requires completion of all stages, the stages do not need to be completed in any particular order or in any set amount of time. A stage can be repeated or revisited a number of times. And, sometimes a stage is completed with little effort, while at other times a stage is difficult and time-consuming.

Knowing where they are in the process is very helpful for students. It helps them to know what's been completed and what is still to do. When working on an assignment, project, report, or even an information problem of personal interest, students should be able to identify where they are in the process. For example, are they reading an article related to current events? That's Use of Information, Big6 #4. Are they searching for sources using a subscription database? That's Big6 #3, Location and Access.

Similarly, teachers should frame instructional and learning experiences related to information and technology skills instruction within the Big6 process. Are they teaching PowerPoint for multimedia presentation? That's Synthesis, Big6 #5. Are students working with the library media specialist to determine possible sources for a project? That's Information Seeking Strategies, Big6 #2.

Anchoring instruction in individual skills within the overall Big6 process provides students with a familiar reference point. They see the connections among seemingly separate skills and are able to reflect on what came before and anticipate what comes after.

Therefore, we recommend continually working with students to help them recognize where they are in the process. Some ways that teachers can do this is by:

- Identifying for students the various Big6 stages as they go through an assignment, project, or report.
- Using a story or video to point out the Big6 stages related to the actions of one or more characters.
- Modeling Big6 process recognition by pointing out when they themselves are engaging in a particular Big6 stage.
- Asking students, verbally or in writing, to identify which Big6 stage they are working on.

Context 2: Curriculum

Information is a pervasive and essential part of our society and our lives. We are, at our essence, processors and users of information. This is not a recent development. Humans have always been dependent upon information to help them make decisions and to guide their actions. The change has come in the sheer volume of information and the complexity of information systems—largely due to advances in information technology and the accelerated rate at which we live.

Information is pervasive, and so are the Big6 information skills. Therefore, there are many opportunities for teaching and learning the Big6 Skills. From research and experience, we know that the Big6 Skills are best learned in the context of real needs—school or personal. Students today, more than ever, want to see connections between what they are learning and their lives. They want to know how something is relevant. This is no problem for the Big6, as the approach emphasizes applicability across environments and situations.

Most often in school settings, the context for Big6 Skills instruction is the actual classroom curriculum. This includes the subject area units and lessons of study, and most importantly, the assignments on which students will be evaluated. Throughout the school year, teachers and students engage in a rich range of curriculum subjects and topics. In fact, one of the current problems we face in education is "curriculum information overload." There is just too much to cover in a limited time.

That is why, in implementing Big6 instruction, we do not promote adding new curriculum content, units, or topics. There is plenty going on in the curriculum already. The last thing that classroom teachers and students need is more content. Therefore, from a Big6 perspective, the challenge is to determine good opportunities for learning and teaching Big6 Skills within the existing curriculum. This involves the following actions:

(1) Analyze the curriculum to (a) select units and assignments that are well-suited to Big6 Skills instruction, and (b) determine which Big6 Skills are particularly relevant to the selected curriculum units and assignments.

(2) Develop a broad plan that links the Big6 to various curriculum units.

(3) Design integrated unit and lesson plans to teach the Big6 in the context of the subject area curriculum.

We strongly advocate a collaborative approach to Big6 Skills instruction. That is, classroom teachers, library media specialists, technology teachers, and other educators can work together to analyze the curriculum, develop a broad plan, and design specific units and lesson plans that integrate the Big6 and classroom content. These educators can also collaborate on teaching and assessment.

Analyzing Curriculum from a Big6 Perspective

Effective Big6 instruction starts with selecting existing curriculum units that are best suited to integrated Big6 Skills instruction. We refer to these units as "big juicies"—those information-rich curriculum units that are dripping with Big6 potential. "Big juicy" units are rich in information needs, resources, and processing. These are the units that offer particularly good opportunities for teaching specific Big6 Skills within the overall Big6 process.

For example, select units that involve a report, project, or product rather than those that rely on a test for assessment. Focus on units that require a range of multiple resources rather than only the textbook. Desirable units should also involve a large number of students and span a reasonable timeframe. Let us see how this might work in practice.

Seventh grade life science teacher Ms. Lowe and library media specialist Mr. Bennett meet to discuss how they might collaborate to help students improve their information problem-solving skills while they study biology. They analyze the major units that Ms. Lowe plans to teach during the school year, and agree that there are three key units because they (1) result in some form of product or project, (2) require many different types of resources, (3) involve the whole class, and (4) span more than just a week or two. In other words, these three units seem to be particularly "information-rich," and are perfect candidates for integrated life science-Big6 instruction. These are their big juicies:

- *The anatomy unit*: taught early in the school year, takes three weeks, involves significant use of the Web, results in individual PowerPoint-supported oral presentations.

- *The circulatory system unit*: taught in the second marking period, takes two weeks, involves a series of worksheets that combine to make a study guide, also requires students to identify structures and functions, and to analyze the effect of oxygenation on various other systems (e.g., nervous system, immune system, digestive system).

- *The digestive system unit*: taught in the third marking period, results in group presentations on the digestive process in different animals, and usually involves extensive information seeking and searching.

What now? Do they select among these units or do they just integrate the Big6 with all three? Do they teach all the Big6 Skills with each unit or focus on specific Big6 Skills?

These choices depend upon other factors, including the time available for Big6 instruction and what else is going on during the school year. We do, however, recommend that while they review and reinforce the overall Big6 process with each unit, Ms. Lowe and Mr. Bennett should provide targeted Big6 Skills instruction on one or two of the specific skills. For example:

- The anatomy unit relies on PowerPoint and the Web, so lessons can be taught on both. PowerPoint is a Synthesis tool, so that's a Big6 #5 lesson focusing on organizing and presenting principles using PowerPoint. Lessons on the Web might focus on identifying useful types of Web sites (Big6 #2: Information Seeking Strategies), using keyword search terms (Big6 #3: Location and Access), and recognizing and extracting relevant information, (Big6 #4: Use of Information).

Look at how many of the Big6 you're focusing on Specifics

- The circulatory system unit might be a good unit in which to focus on Big6 #1: Task Definition, because each worksheet has a different focus. There is also a great deal of targeted analysis, so Big6 #4: Use of Information, is again important.

- The digestive system unit is a group project and comes later in the school year. This would be a good opportunity to review the entire Big6 process while emphasizing defining tasks and dividing up the work (Big6 #1: Task Definition) and how to put group presentations together so they make sense and flow easily (Big6 #5: Synthesis). Evaluation (Big6 #6) can also play a big role in group projects as students may be required to judge themselves and other group members or to assess the final products of other groups.

In actual school settings, selecting units for integrated Big6 instruction and overall Big6 Skills planning depends upon the specific needs of the students as well as the setting and situation. The ultimate goal is to provide frequent opportunities for students to learn and practice the Big6. Repetition is crucial. While these skills may seem to be simple or common sense at first, they actually are quite involved and can be difficult to master. We cannot overstress this point: we learn through repetition. It is not enough to teach each Big6 Skill or sub-skill once. Students' proficiency with specific Big6 Skills, as well as the overall process, will improve over time if they have regular opportunities to learn and to apply the Big6.

Planning for Big6 learning will differ based upon the situation, curriculum, setting, and who is going to be involved, e.g., the classroom teacher, library media specialist, teaching team, technology teacher, entire grade level or subject area, school, or district. Examples of each of these situations are presented below.

Planning and Plans for the Individual Teacher

Classroom teachers typically organize and plan the school year around a series of curriculum units and lessons. Based on local or state curriculum guides, teachers determine the sequence of units, their general goals and objectives, and the time they will spend on each unit. While they frequently make adjustments during the school year, most teachers try to cover the intended units in sequence.

As described above, we suggest that teachers review the existing curriculum plans to determine opportunities to integrate Big6 Skills instruction. The task is to first identify units that have good potential for integrating Big6 Skills and then decide which Big6 Skills to emphasize with each unit.

Units that are good candidates for integrating Big6 Skills instruction generally:

- Are of longer duration
- Involve a report, project, or product rather than a quiz or test

- Use multiple resources
- Involve a range of teaching methods.

As noted, it is not necessary or desirable to teach all stages of the Big6 with each curriculum unit. The Big6 is applicable to any problem-solving situation, so students will have ample opportunity to work on the Big6 throughout the school year. Therefore, when students are first presented with an assignment as part of a curriculum unit, we recommend first "talking through" the assignment in the context of the overall Big6 process. Then, as students work through the assignment, the teacher, often in partnership with the library media specialist and technology teacher, can offer more in depth lessons on one or more of the Big6 Skills. By the end of the school year, students in the class should have experienced a full range of Big6 lessons in the context of the real curriculum and the overall Big6 process.

Figure 4.1 is a sample "Big6 Skills by Unit Matrix" for Ms. Yacono, a social studies teacher with classes in U.S. history. The matrix is an efficient way to summarize Ms. Yacono's integrated Big6 plans. (Note: The plans included here are composites of a number of teachers and settings. They do not actually refer to any specific school, district, or teacher.)

Figure 4.1 documents the units that Ms. Yacono intends to integrate with Big6 Skills instruction. The units are sorted chronologically in terms of Marking Period (M_Per), which notes the order they will be introduced in the school year. Information is also included on assignments and Big6 Skills targeted for in-depth instruction. A large X indicates that a Big6 lesson will be taught while a small x indicates that the Big6 Skill will only be touched on.

For example, the first U.S. history unit is about Colonial America, which is taught in the first marking period. This is a textbook-based unit, and the assignments are introductory—a timeline and a test. The Big6 lesson relates to Big6 #4: Use of Information, focusing on effective and efficient use of textbook information. Ms. Yacono will also mention Big6 #1: Task Definition, by helping students to learn that it is their responsibility to ask about the scope and format of the test.

From Figure 4.1, we also see that Ms. Yacono uses the U.S. Constitution unit as a major kickoff to the Big6 process during the second marking period. Here, she and the library media specialist will teach lessons on each of the Big6 as students go through the process. Ms. Yacono will also introduce technology skills within the Big6 process in the U.S. Constitution unit, particularly the use of the Web and other digital resources, PowerPoint presentation software, and e-mail. Ms. Yacono returns to these integrated technology skills in the map skills unit at the end of the year.

If developed at the beginning of the school year, the Big6 Skills by Unit Matrix became a blueprint for integrated information skills instruction. It can also be updated during the year to reflect what actually takes place. Therefore, at the end of the year, the matrix offers detailed documentation of

Figure 4.1: Big6 Skills by Unit Matrix: Ms. Yacono—Social Studies

GR	UNIT	ASSIGNMENT	M_PER	1	2	3	4	5	6	TECHNOLOGY	COMMENTS
8	Colonial America 13 colonies	timeline, test	1xxx	X	X	X	X	x	X	WWW, subscription databases	
8	Revolutionary Era notable individuals	report, presentation	1xxx	x			X				use of textbook
8	U.S. Constitution	project	x2xx	X	X	X	X	X	X	WWW, subscription databases, word processing	major reports–all Big6
8	early republic War of 1812	chart–events and markets	x2xx		X	X		X			focus on analysis
8	Westward Expansion Manifest Destiny	report	xx3x		X	X				WWW, subscription databases	
8	Civil War: Slavery 20s & 30s	audio project	xx3x	X			X	X		audio recording/podcast	groups do two radio news shows
8	Reconstruction: social problems	project	xxx4	X							major project–Big6 focus printed or Web–based
8	Map skills	create maps	xxx4	X	x	x	x	X	X	WWW, subscription databases, mapping software	

what was actually accomplished. The plans also serve as the basis for follow-up planning by the teacher for the next year and for other teachers who will have the same students the next year.

Planning and Plans for a Subject Area, Grade, or Team

While Big6 implementation through individual teachers is essential, it is also valuable to coordinate Big6 Skills instruction in broader contexts. This section explains how this can happen within a particular subject area, grade, or team.

Figure 4.2 offers a sample Big6 Skills by Unit Matrix for a middle school social studies department. The data included are similar to Figure 4.1; however, we have added columns for Grade and Teacher.

On the plan, we see that in the sixth grade, Ms. Sullivan (TJS), intends to focus on the Big6 in three units. In the first marking period, the class studies Medieval Europe and the unit culminates in a project. Since this is the beginning of the school year, Ms. Sullivan will quickly review the overall Big6 process, but will develop lessons that focus on:

- Task Definition: understanding what is expected on her tests.
- Synthesis: developing strategies for writing short essays on tests.
- Evaluation: recognizing the criteria for success including which topics and concepts are more or less important.

Ms. Sullivan, the library media specialist, and technology teacher will deliver other Big6 lessons during the school year. For example, the library media specialist will provide a lesson about selecting, locating, and using quality information sources particularly in relation to the World Wide Web (Big6 #2, #3, #4) for the Byzantine Empire unit, and the technology teacher will offer instruction on special software for creating computer-generated maps (Big6 #5) for the unit on native cultures.

The matrix documents similar intentions by other teachers. The plan for Ms. Yacono (REY) was discussed in the previous section.

Mr. Robinson in seventh grade state history is a major Big6 "fan" and he plans to integrate Big6 instruction across several units. Again, as with Ms. Sullivan, he will focus on one or two of the Big6 within a given unit, but by the end of the year he will have covered all six stages in depth.

Figure 4.3 focuses on grade seven, and indicates Big6 units throughout the year. The matrix also helps to compare across teachers to determine possible areas for collaboration and to help avoid conflicting demands for resources.

For example, we see that the health teacher, Ms. Rausch (CER), teaches three major units with Big6 connections. Health is a one-half year course, so the units actually are repeated twice and eventually includes all students. Therefore, these are excellent units for Big6 instruction. Ms. Rausch teaches all of the Big6 with a particular emphasis on technology.

Figure 4.2 Social Studies Department by Grade and Teacher

The Big6

GR	TCHR	UNIT	ASSIGNMENT	M_PER	1	2	3	4	5	6	TECHNOLOGY	COMMENTS
6	TJS	Byzantine Empire	product	x23x	X	X	X	x	X	x	WWW, electronic resources, word processing, present, e-mail	lots of technology
6	CGR	Contributions of Individuals	test, short written assignment, project	1xxx			X				WWW, word processing	
6	HJW	Map Skills	demonstrations and illustrations	1xxx		x		X				use of maps
6	TJS	Medieval Europe	test	1xxx	X	x	x	x	X	X		test taking strategies–task definition, synthesis
6	TJS	Major Contributors	report	x2xx	X	X	x	X	X	x	WWW, electronic resources	sources–Web searching, note taking
7	TJS	Native Cultures	maps, product	xx3x					X		present, graphing software	computer software to create various kinds of maps
7	ALR	Notable Individuals in the Founding of the State	report	x2xx	X	X		X	X	X	WWW, electronic resources, word processing, present, e-mail	major reports—all Big6
7	ALR	State Government	project	xx3x		X	X		X			
7	ALR	Important Economic Factors in the State Today	project	xxx4	X		X		X		WWW, electronic resources, word processing	
7	WAJ	Geography of the State	written and oral report	x2xx					X	X	present, word processing	PowerPoint
7	WAJ	Diverse Cultures	displays	xx3x	X							nature of test
8	REY	Colonial America: the 13 Colonies	timeline	1xxx	X	X	X	X		X	WWW, subscription databases	use of textbook
8	REY	Revolutionary Era: Notable Individuals	report, project	1xxx	x			X				
8	REY	U. S. Constitution	project	x2xx	X	X	X	X	X	X	WWW, subscription databases, word processing	major project—all Big6
8	REY	Early Republic War of 1812	chart - events and markets	x2xx				X		X		focus on analysis
8	REY	Westward Expansion: Manifest Destiny	report	xx3x		x	x				WWW, subscription databases	
8	REY	Civil War Slavery	audio project	xx3x	X			X	X		audio recording/podcast	groups do two radio news shows
8	REY	Reconstruction: Social Problems	project	xx3x	X							major project—Big6 focus, printed or Web-based
8	REY	Map Skills	create maps	xx3x	X	x		x	X	Xx	WWW, subscription databases	

Figure 4.3 Units Open to Seventh Grade Students

The Big6

GR	TCHR	UNIT	SUBJECT	ASSIGNMENT	M_PER	1	2	3	4	5	6	TECHNOLOGY	COMMENTS
7	NOU	Career	Drama	report, project	xx3x	X	x	x		X		WWW, electronic resources	
7	CER	Diet & Nutrition	Health	posters	1x3x	X	X	x	X	X	x	WWW, PowerPoint 2x year, stress critical evaluation of info	all students take health; repeats
7	CER	Tobacco & Smoking	Health	test	1x3x	X					X	strategies & the Big6	cooperative teacher, test-taking
7	CER	Drugs	Health	product	x2x4	X	x	x	X	x	X	WWW, electronic resources, word processing, present	
7	ALR	Native Cultures of the State	SS–State History	maps, product	xx3x					X		present, graphing software various kinds of maps	computer software to create
7	ALR	Notable Individuals in the Founding of the State	SS–State History	report	x2xx	X	X	X	X	X	X	WWW, electronic resources, word processing	major reports—all Big6
7	ALR	State Government	SS–State History	project	xx3x		x	x				WWW	Web-based information
7	ALR	Important Economic Factors in the State Today	SS–State History	project	xxx4	X				X		WWW, electronic resources, word processing	
7	WAJ	Geography of the State	SS–State History	written and oral reports	x2xx		x			X		present, word processing	PowerPoint
7	WAJ	Diverse Cultures	SS–State History	displays	xx3x	X							nature of test
7	RBW	Light Lab	Science	lab report, test	xx3x					X		spreadsheets	
7	MAB	Spanish Cooking	Spanish I	product	xxx4	X	X	X				WWW, electronic resources, word processing	
7	BAJ	Influence of TV, Theatre and Film in Daily Life	Fine Arts	project	1234	X	X	X	X	X	X	WWW, electronic resources intelligence	full year, competitive
7	WED	Persuasive Paper	English language arts	letters to city council	xx3x	x	x	x	x	X	X	WWW, electronic resources, word processing	major project—Big6 focus printed or Web-based
7	WED	Historical Novels—Fact or Fiction?	English language arts	analysis of "facts" in novels	xxx4	x	x	x	X	x	x	WWW, electronic resources, word processing, present, graphics, e-mail	

One of her major concerns is that students learn to think critically about health information sources, so she focuses on Big6 #4: Use of Information in all her units.

Mr. Robinson (ALR), Mrs. Wilson (RBW), and Mrs. Bonzi (MAB) also plan to integrate the Big6 and technology into their subject area units for the first time. Mr. Robinson wants students to dig out unique information from sources for their study of notable individuals. Mrs. Wilson will teach students how to use electronic spreadsheets to organize and present their laboratory results (Big6 #5: Synthesis). Mrs. Bonzi will have students use the Web and other digital resources to search for recipes and background information for her Spanish cooking unit (Big6 #2: Information Seeking Strategies and Big6 #3: Location and Access).

Figure 4.3 is also useful for highlighting common units and time frames. We see that Mr. Johnson (WAJ), Mr. Dominguez (WED), and Mr. Robinson are all teaching the Big6 in the third marking period to seventh grade students. Some students may be in two or all three classes. And, if the students are also in health, they may receive Big6 instruction from Ms. Rausch as well! This might be too much, so the teachers may want to compare notes so they minimize duplication.

Planning and Plans on the School Level

It is also important to plan for systematic Big6 Skills instruction at the school level. The goal is to ensure that students have a range of Big6 instructional experiences across grade levels and subjects. These experiences should build upon each other so that by the end of their K-12 education, each student has had ample opportunities to develop competencies in specific technology and information skills within the overall Big6 context.

Library Media Specialist as Big6 Coordinator

School-wide Big6 planning requires cooperation among classroom teachers, library media specialists, technology teachers, and administrators. From experience, we find that active, engaged library media specialists are in an ideal position to coordinate the school-wide Big6 Skills effort. First, information skills instruction is a major function of library media programs. In addition, library media specialists are involved with instruction across the curriculum. They are responsible for providing resources and services to all grades and subjects and generally have an excellent overview of the existing school curriculum. Therefore, we recommend, when possible, that library media specialists coordinate Big6 planning with technology teachers, classroom teachers, administrators, and support staff.

Figure 4.4 is a partially completed Big6 by Unit Matrix for a middle school covering grades six through eight. At this point, the matrix only includes some of the units slated for integrated Big6 instruction. The library media

Figure 4.4: Big6 Skills by Unit Matrix: Middle School

The Big6

GR	TCHR	UNIT	SUBJECT	ASSIGNMENT	M_PER	1	2	3	4	5	6	TECHNOLOGY	COMMENTS
6	TMJ	Weather	Sci	test	xx3x	x			x		x		
6	TCH	Recycling	Social Studies	product	x23x		x	x	x	x	x	WWW, electronic resources, word processing, present, e-mail	lots of technology
6	RTD	Mysteries	English	video	1xxx	x				x			
6	TMJ	Noise	Sci. General	written report	x2xx	x	x	x	x	x	x	WWW, electronic resources, word processing, present, e-mail	build on gr 7, technology
6	CGR	Rainforest	Social Studies	test, short written assignment, project	1xxx	x		x	x			WWW, word processing	
7	RTD	Notable Individuals in the Founding of the State	Social Studies	report	1xxx	x			x				use of maps
7	TJS	Latin America	Area Studies	test	1xxx	x				x	x		test taking strategies- task definition, synthesis
7	TJS	Northern Africa	Area Studies	test, report	x2xx		x	x	x	x	x	WWW, electronic resources	sources, Web searching, note-taking
7	BAJ	Influence of TV, Theatre and Film in Daily American Life	Fine Arts	ongoing project	1234	x	x	x	x	x	x	WWW, electronic resources	full-year, competitive intelligence
7	NOU	Career	Drama	report, project	xx3x	x	x	x		x	x	WWW, electronic resources	
7	CER	Diet & Nutrition	Health	posters	1x3x	x	x	x		x	x	WWW, PowerPoint	all students take health; repeats 2x year, stress critical evaluation of info
8	CER	Tobacco & Smoking	Health	test	1x3x	x			x	x	x		cooperative teacher, test-taking strategies & the Big6
8	CER	Drugs	Health	product	x2x4	x	x	x	x	x	x	WWW, electronic resources, word processing, present	full year, competitive
8	MBE	Web Authoring	Library	product (Web page)	x2xx	x	x	x		x		Front Page, HTML, scanner	
8	REY	U. S. Constitution	Social Studies	x2xx	x2xx	x	x	x	x	x	x	WWW, subscription databases, word processing	major project—all Big6
8	REY	Map Skills	Social Studies	create maps	xxx4	x	x	x	x	x	x	WWW, subscription databases, mapping software	
8	CAL	Recycling	Earth Science	posters	x2xx	x			x				compile worksheets, targeted analysis
8	REY	Colonial America: the 13 Colonies	Social Studies	timeline, project	1xxx	x	x	x	x	x	x	WWW, subscription databases	review Big6

specialist is compiling this plan, and has worked on documenting integrated units across the grade levels and subject areas. The units that involve extensive Big6 instruction with three or more planned Big6 lessons are:

- 7th grade—recycling—social studies
- 6th grade—noise—science
- 7th grade—Latin America—social studies
- 7th grade—influence of TV—fine arts
- 7th grade—diet and nutrition—health
- 8th grade—drugs—health
- 8th grade—U.S. Constitution—social studies
- 8th grade—map skills—social studies
- 8th grade—Colonial America—social studies

These extensive units are supplemented by Big6 instruction in other classes as well. However, there is still room for expansion of the integrated information and technology skills instructional program. Expanded collaboration among teachers can be coordinated by the library media specialist and technology teachers. The goal is to expand this plan to ensure that all students have formal opportunities to learn Big6 and technology skills. The matrix is a useful planning tool for this, and later it becomes the documentation for the implemented program.

Summary

Systematic planning for integrated Big6 Skills instruction is essential if we are to make a difference in our classrooms and schools. If we truly believe that information and technology skills are essential for student success, then we must make sure that students have frequent opportunities to learn and practice these skills.

It is not enough to work with students one-on-one or to offer an isolated lesson in note taking or Web search engines. Students need lessons in each of the Big6 Skills, delivered in the context of real subject area assignments. Accomplishing comprehensive, integrated Big6 instruction requires classroom teachers, library media specialists, technology teachers, and administrators to make a concerted and systematic effort to plan and document their efforts.

Figure 4.5 is a blank Big6 Skills by Unit Matrix to help you get started.

Figure 4.5: Blank Big6 Skills by Unit Matrix

The Big6™

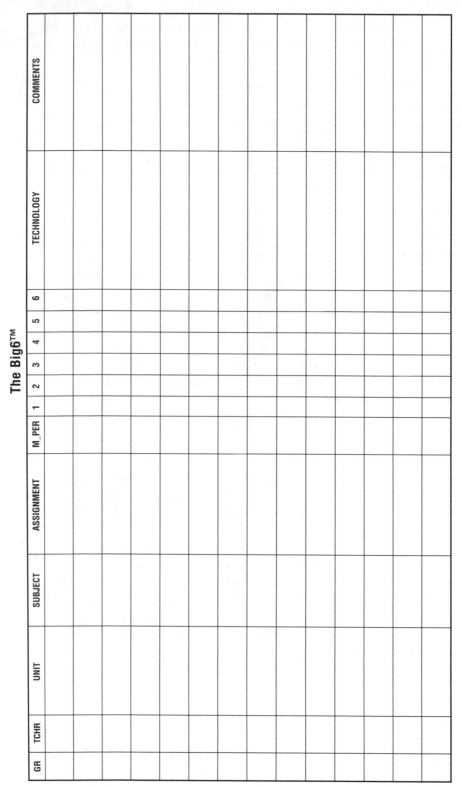

GR	TCHR	UNIT	SUBJECT	ASSIGNMENT	M_PER	1	2	3	4	5	6	TECHNOLOGY	COMMENTS

Chapter 5

Assessment of Information & Technology Skills

Introduction

While not always the most enjoyable part of learning and teaching, assessment is nevertheless essential to helping students attain higher levels of achievement. This is particularly important in relation to the Big6, as we believe that competence in information problem solving is a key to success in every curriculum area.

By assessing students' skills in each of the Big6, we can pinpoint strengths and weaknesses and target areas for further development. We can also assess how well students are able to apply the Big6 process to a range of tasks and offer additional instruction as necessary.

Effective assessment should do three things:

- Communicate teacher expectations.
- Provide motivation.
- Enable students to assess themselves.

To do so, educators should consider the following:

- The specific content-learning goals.
- Related Big6 Skills.
- Criteria for assessment.
- Evidence to examine to determine student performance.

Assessment that focuses on instructional objectives and is based on established criteria helps teachers to appropriately modify and target instruction. Assessment can also help educators determine whether students are eligible for advanced instruction or if students need special, individualized assistance.

Assessment can be defined as making judgments based on a predetermined set of criteria. From a Big6 perspective, two broad criteria for assessment are effectiveness and efficiency.

Effectiveness and Efficiency

Two key criteria of assessment are part of Stage 6: Evaluation in the Big6 process:

#6.1 Effectiveness of the product.
#6.2 Efficiency of the process.

Students learn to assess the results of their efforts by analyzing the effectiveness of their product and their efficient use of the Big6 process to complete various tasks and create various products. Even young children can learn to judge whether they are effective (having done a good job or worthy of a good grade) or efficient (not wasting time and effort). As students get older, they can assume more and more responsibility for their own achievement and assessment of that achievement.

In relation to effectiveness, students can learn to judge their own products. Students can diagnose the result of their effort when they learn to do such things as the following:

- Compare the requirements to the results.

- Check the appropriateness and accuracy of the information they use.

- Judge how well their solution is organized.

- Rate the quality of their final product or performance compared to their potential (i.e., Did I do the best that I could?).

- Judge the quality of their product to a predefined standard.

These, of course, are rather sophisticated actions. Less sophisticated learners can still ask themselves such questions as:

- Is my project good; how do I know?

- Am I proud of my project?

Assessing efficiency requires students to evaluate the nature, tendencies, and preferences of their personal information problem-solving process. This is sometimes referred to as metacognition—recognizing how we learn, process information, and solve problems. With the Big6, we can help students learn how to assess the efficiency of the process they use to reach decisions and solutions. Some assessment techniques to facilitate this include the following:

- Keeping and evaluating a log of activities.

- Reflecting back on the sequence of events and judging effort and time involved.

- Reviewing and analyzing the areas of frustration and barriers they encountered.

- Rating their abilities to perform specific information problem-solving actions (e.g., locating, note taking, skimming, scanning, prioritizing).

Simply stated, students can begin by asking themselves the following:

- Am I pleased with my effort?

- What was easy and what was difficult?

- How could I do better next time?

These are the types of questions that teachers can build into activities and assignments.

Forms and Context for Assessment

There are two broad forms of assessment—**summative** and **formative**. Summative is after-the-fact assessment, designed to determine the degree of student learning after they have completed a lesson, unit, or other instructional event. Assessing students' performance on the overall information problem-solving process through a project, report, or assignment, for example, is summative assessment. Formative assessment involves providing feedback so that adjustments can be made before students turn in their work. Formative assessment of information and technology skills might involve assessing students' work at each stage of the Big6. Classroom teachers, library media specialists, and other educators can either provide feedback at each step of the information problem-solving process—when the assignment, project, or product is completed—or both.

Throughout this book, we emphasize that the Big6 Skills are best learned in the context of real curriculum needs. School curriculum is rich and detailed at all grade levels, and Big6 Skills instruction can easily be integrated with a range of subjects and topics. Assessment of Big6 Skills is similarly best conducted within real curriculum contexts. That means finding ways to determine students' abilities in the overall process and individual Big6 Skills as they complete various homework assignments, projects, reports, products, and tests.

Most often, the focus of assessment is on evaluating how well students are doing with just the classroom content. Content learning is clearly of major importance. But, we must also be concerned with process skills as embodied by the Big6. How effective and efficient are students overall and in the specific skills necessary to solve information problems? Effective assessment speaks to many audiences:

- To students—to let them know how they are doing and how they can improve.

- To teachers—to help them determine whether students are learning the content and skills and if they need to reteach.

- To parents—to keep them informed about the level of success of their children and how they might help them.

Assessment should measure performance in a manner that is easily understood by all audiences. In addition, good assessment strategies do the following:

- Reflect the objectives of the lesson or unit.
- Measure the behavior described by the objective.
- Make certain that students fully understand all assessment criteria.
- Provide constructive feedback on strengths and weaknesses.

Ways of Assessing

Assessing the Big6 Skills in context includes the following key elements:

- Evidence to examine to determine student performance.
- The specific content-learning goals.
- Related Big6 Skills.
- Criteria for judging.
- A rating scale for judging.
- The judgments themselves.

Each element is essential to successful assessment and is explained in more detail below.

Evidence

As stated, assessment of Big6 Skills should take place within the context of real curriculum needs. In practice, that means looking carefully at assignments. For a given curriculum unit, teachers select one or more assignments to emphasize the importance of content and skills, to motivate students and to evaluate student performance. In most instances, assignments will comprise the "evidence" of assessing Big6 learning. Other options include observing student performance, talking to students during or after working on an assignment, or having students engage in self-assessment activities. Typical assignments include the following:

- Homework other than worksheets
- Worksheets
- Exercises
- Reports or research papers
- Projects
- Quizzes or tests

Figure 5.1: Sample Criteria Statements for the Big6™

Task Definition
The student demonstrates the ability to:
- Determine the information problem to be solved
- Clearly define the task
- Identify the important elements of the task
- Show complete understanding of the task and its parts
- Pick out keywords embedded in a question
- Ask good questions
- Understand and follow printed and oral directions.

Information Seeking Strategies
The student demonstrates the ability to:
- Develop an approach to seeking a variety of materials
- Determine which information sources are most/least important
- Determine which information sources are most/least appropriate
- Demonstrate knowledge of relevant sources
- Recognize that information can be gained from many sources including investigation and observation
- Understand the value of human resources
- Use appropriate criteria for selecting sources, including readability, scope, authority, currency, usefulness, and format.

Location & Access
The student demonstrates the ability to:
- Gather resources independently
- Ask questions to obtain information
- Determine what sources are available
- Access appropriate information systems, including: online subscription databases, catalog-master list, and electronic multimedia.

Use of Information
The student demonstrates the ability to:
- Paraphrase the main idea accurately from written, visual and oral source material
- Summarize the main idea from written, visual and oral source material
- Distinguish facts from opinions
- Gather information carefully (read, listen, and view)
- Cite sources accurately.

Synthesis
The student demonstrates the ability to:
- Prepare an accurate bibliography of all resources (Internet and other resources)
- Organize information
- Present information
- Use a standard bibliographic format
- Prepare charts, graphs, outlines
- Compare and contrast points of view from several sources
- Summarize and retell information from multiple sources
- Design products to communicate content.

Evaluation
The student demonstrates the ability to:
- Assess projects for strengths and weaknesses
- Provide recommendations for improving the information problem-solving result
- Judge solutions and decisions
- Assess the completeness of the response to the assigned task
- Review and critique the steps used in solving an information problem.

Content Learning Goals

Content learning goals include the skills and topics of the subject area curriculum. These can be established by individual classroom teachers or designated by a standard curriculum at the school, district, region, or state level.

Big6 Learning Goals

It is not necessary or desirable to assess all the Big6 in every assignment. In fact, it can become tedious to do so. Therefore, we encourage educators to focus assessment on the Big6 Skills that were (1) taught, or (2) particularly important to the learning and assignment.

Criteria for Judging

Assessment criteria should be clearly defined statements of intended learner outcomes. Criteria should describe competence levels and should be designed to measure students' achievement toward instructional goals. For the Big6 Skills, criteria should relate to students' abilities in applying the Big6 to the content learning goals. To assist teachers, sample criteria statements for each stage of the Big6 are provided in Figure 5.1.

A Rating Scale for Judging

Rating scales are used as an indication of a student's learning state on criteria at a given point in time. The scale can be a simple numbered order, labels, or even symbols:

Figure 5.2 Rating Scale

Low			High
1	2	3	4
Needs work	Okay	Well done	Super
Oops! See me, please.	You did 3/5 requirements far!	One more draft, please.	Bravo!

The less able the students, the more we suggest avoiding any numerical scales. The main point is that teachers and students need to have a simple way to express the learning state.

The Judgments

To make developing and implementing judgments easier, we created Big6 Scoring Guides. These guides combine the various elements of assessment in a straightforward form. In the next section, we create Big6 Scoring Guides and give specific examples of how to use a scoring guide.

Big6 Scoring Guides

In addition to pulling together all the requisite elements of assessment, Big6 Scoring Guides are designed to communicate teachers' expectations for students' work in ways that students can understand and use. Big6 Scoring Guides focus on the information problem-solving process as well as the final result. Therefore, guides are useful both during and after working on assignments—for both formative and summative assessment.

Formative assessment involves diagnosing students' performance during learning so that adjustments can be made before students turn in their work. Adjustments may include the following:

- Redirecting planned instruction to focus on areas where students are having trouble.

- Providing special learning activities not previously planned.

- Helping students to apply relevant technology tools.

- Redefining the problem or returning to a previous Big6 stage.

- Offering one-on-one tutoring.

- Brainstorming alternative approaches.

These types of adjustments are prescriptions for improving learning. Of course, Big6 Scoring Guides can also be used to assess final products—summative assessment. Many teachers find that post-assignment debriefings built around Big6 Scoring Guides are effective ways to involve students in the assessment process.

It is relatively easy to create and use a Big6 Scoring Guide:

1. Define the curriculum objectives within a Big6 context.

2. Determine which Big6 Skills are important (the focus) for the particular assignment.

3. Develop criteria across a scale (e.g., from "highly competent" to "not yet acceptable"). There may be more than one aspect to each criterion. Consider which aspects are essential.

4. Determine what evidence will be examined to determine student performance for each Big6 Skill.

5. Conduct the assessment.

6. Share the assessment with students.

7. Determine and document the level of achievement.

8. Revise as necessary.

For example, assume that completing the worksheet in Figure 5.3 is the task for students in seventh grade biology studying "muscular activity."

Figure 5.4 is the Big6 Scoring Guide designed to assess students' performance. This guide is designed to include multiple assessments—by student (S), teacher (T), or library media specialist (L). This allows students and teachers to quickly identify gaps in their views of perceived performance. Focusing on gaps can lead to clarification of misunderstandings and highlighting the need for further instruction.

The column labeled "Evidence" is used to indicate the products or techniques to be used to assess specific skills. Examples of evidence include written, visual, multimedia, or oral products, assignments, homework, projects, tests, observation, or even self-reflection. This is an essential piece of the Scoring Guide because it identifies the specific context for assessing student performance.

The last column, "Focus," relates to the relative importance of each skill being evaluated. It is not necessary or desirable to assess all Big6 Skills equally in every learning situation. The assigned focus should be based on the goals and objectives of the unit in terms of Big6 skill development and content learning. For example, in the muscle example, a percentage of emphasis is assigned to each of the Big6. Location and Access is not a skill emphasized in this situation while the focus is on Task Definition and Synthesis.

Self-Assessment

Continuous self-assessment is an integral part of the Big6. When students engage in Big6 #6 Evaluation activities, they are conducting self-assessment. In addition to having students reflect on their own abilities, self-assessment fosters independence and responsibility in students. Through self-assessment, students learn to translate expectations into action, build on their accomplishments, and work on weaknesses. Yet it is important to remember that students are better able to assess their work when they have a scoring system. This system may resemble a teacher's scoring guide. It can be as simple as a checklist of the required elements for the assignment. It can be more complicated, asking students to grade themselves and provide a rationale. As teachers, you need to consider your own and your students' needs for appropriate assessment tools.

Teachers can reinforce self-assessment by involving students in developing criteria, grading schemes, and Big6 Scoring Guides. Teachers can also help students to generalize from "schoolwork assessment" (e.g., on projects, tests, assignments) to success in areas of personal interest (e.g., sports, art, music, hobbies), and ultimately at work (e.g., job satisfaction, salary, making a contribution).

It is difficult, if not impossible, for students to do their best if they don't know how to recognize it when they see it. All too often, students are left to guess at such things as whether they are finished with an assignment or whether they have done a good job on an assignment. Students should be able to compare their efforts with their teachers' expectations and with established standards. When necessary, students need to revise or redirect their effort. And, self-assessment may result in students realizing that they need to learn new skills.

Seventh Grade Science Laboratory Experiment:
Muscular Action Worksheet

Your task is to design a controlled experiment to test the hypothesis below. Your experiment should be designed so that it can be conducted in a 15 to 20 minute period.

Hypothesis:

When there is an increase in muscular activity, there is a corresponding increase in the energy used by muscles. This energy increase causes heat as well as a corresponding increase in oxygen consumption.

Material:

Procedure:

Result: (tabulate data and represent in an appropriate graph)

Conclusion:

Questions:
- What variable(s) did you test?
- What are the constants?
- What was the experimental control?
- Evaluation/Scoring Guide

Figure 5.4: Science Lab Scoring Guide

Criteria

Big6 Skills	Highly Competent 10 points	Competent 8 points	Adequate 7 points	Not Yet Acceptable 5 points	Evidence	Focus
Eisenberg/Berkowitz © 1988						
1. Task Definition 1.1 Define the problem. 1.2 Identify the information needed.	Experiment meets 15-20 minute requirements. Procedure tested: oxygen consumption & levels of heat. — S T L	Experiment limited to 15-20 minute requirement. Procedure tested: oxygen consumption or levels of heat. — S T L	Experiment did not meet time requirement. Procedure tested: oxygen consumption or level of heat, but not both. — S T L	Experiment did not meet time requirement. Procedure did not test for either: oxygen consumption or levels of heat. — S T L	Experiment	20%
2. Information Seeking Strategies 2.1 Determine all possible sources. 2.2 Select the best sources.	Procedure can be repeated exactly and produce the same results. Procedure tests the hypothesis. — S T L	Procedure tested the hypothesis, but is not easily followed. — S T L	Procedure tests the hypothesis but is not easily followed, and does not give the same results. — S T L	Procedure does not test the hypothesis. Procedure cannot be repeated at all. — S T L	Procedure	40%
3. Location & Access 3.1 Locate sources. 3.2 Find information within sources.	S T L		S T L	S T L		
4. Use of Information 4.1 Engage (e.g., read hear, view). 4.2 Extract relevant information.	Complete and accurate data tables. Complete and accurate graphs. — S T L	Accurate data tables. Appropriate but incomplete graphs. — S T L	Incomplete data tables. Incomplete and inaccurate graphs. — S T L	No data tables. No graphs. — S T L	Results	10%
5. Synthesis 5.1 Organize information from multiple sources. 5.2 Present the result.	Appropriate conclusion. Answers all questions completely. — S T L	Appropriate conclusion. Answers all questions poorly. — S T L	Conclusion attempted, but is inappropriate. Questions poorly answered and only some questions answered. — S T L	No Conclusion. No questions answered. — S T L	Conclusion Question	20%
6. Evaluation 6.1 Judge the result. (effectiveness). 6.2 Judge the process.	Scoring Guide thoughtfully completed. — S T L	S T L	S T L	Scoring Guide not completed. — S T L	Scoring Guide	10%

We believe it is crucial to help students to learn to do the following:

- Assess their own information problem-solving styles.
- Value and recognize quality work.
- Reflect on the ways they go about tackling assignments and tasks.
- Determine how they can improve.
- Learn how to establish criteria to evaluate their results.

Students often do not take the initiative to self-assess because they have not been encouraged to do so, may not see the value in self-assessment, or may not know how. That is where the Big6 approach comes in. The Big6 reminds us that evaluation is essential to the process. Teachers must prepare students to learn self-assessment in the context of curriculum, personal, or work situations.

Feelings are an important part of self-assessment. Students may lack confidence and pride in their work because they do not really know if they have done a good job. Sometimes, feelings of confidence and pride are replaced with frustration and disappointment when students get their assignment back with a poor grade when they expected to do well. Self-assessment helps students and teachers to apply the same evaluation criteria to the students' work. Students learn to look at their work through their teachers' eyes. In this way, students can build on strengths and identify areas for improvement. Students gain insight into specific areas to improve their performance. This can boost confidence, pride, and encourage a higher level of academic success.

We often assume that students are able to rate the quality of their products or the effectiveness of their information problem-solving approach, but this is not always the case. Self-assessment skills should not be assumed— they should be part of the instructional program. Students need to learn, recognize, and apply the standards of excellence. Again, it is helping students to learn to view their own work in the way teachers view students' work.

Summary

Assessment is an important part of learning and essential to the learning of Big6 Skills. As with Big6 Skills instruction, Big6 assessment should be integrated with classroom curriculum. Existing assignments provide ample opportunities to assess individual Big6 Skills as well as overall information problem-solving abilities. There are requisite elements to assessment that are pulled together in the Big6 Scoring Guides. We include a blank scoring guide (Figure 5.5) to help you get started.

This blank guide is designed to include multiple assessments—by student (S), teacher (T), or library media specialist (L). This allows students and teachers to quickly identify gaps in their views of perceived performance. Focusing on gaps can lead to clarification of misunderstandings and highlighting the need for further instruction.

Figure 5.5: Blank Big6 Scoring Guide

Big6 Assessment Scoring Guide

		Criteria								
Big6™ Skills		**Highly Competent**		**Competent**		**Adequate**		**Not Yet Acceptable**	**Evidence**	**Focus**
Eisenberg/Berkowitz © 1997		**10 points**		**8 points**		**7 points**		**5 points**		
1. Task Definition 1.1 Define the problem. 1.2 Identify the information needed.	S T L		S T L		S T L		S T L			
2. Information Seeking Strategies 2.1 Determine all possible sources. 2.2 Select the best sources.	S T L		S T L		S T L		S T L			
3. Location & Access 3.1 Locate sources. 3.2 Find information within sources.	S T L		S T L		S T L		S T L			
4. Use of Information 4.1 Engage (e.g., read hear, view, and touch). 4.2 Extract relevant information.	S T L		S T L		S T L		S T L			
5. Synthesis 5.1 Organize information from multiple sources. 5.2 Present the result.	S T L		S T L		S T L		S T L			
6. Evaluation 6.1 Judge the result. 6.2 Judge the process.	S T L		S T L		S T L		S T L			

The column labeled "Evidence" is used to indicate the products or techniques to be used to assess specific skills. Examples of evidence include written, visual, or oral products, assignments, homework, projects, tests, observation, or even self-reflection. This is an essential piece of the Scoring Guide because it identifies the specific context for assessing student performance.

The last column, "Focus," relates to the relative importance of each skill being evaluated. It is not necessary or desirable to assess all Big6 Skills equally in every learning situation. The assigned focus should be based on the goals and objectives of the unit in terms of Big6 Skill development and content learning.

Part II: Big6 in Action

by Barbara A. Jansen

Introduction

The first section of this book sets out the theoretical framework of the Big6, and, in general terms, describes how it is applied in various contexts in middle schools, including grades five and nine. This is certainly valuable, but teachers also want to see how the Big6 works in real classroom situations. That is the purpose of Part II: to present the Big6 in action through further explanations and strategies to get started and maintain skills.

Part II is organized around each step of the Big6. Each chapter (6 through 11) explains each step and provides strategies for planning and delivering instruction to students. The strategies are aimed at grades five through nine; however, not all will be appropriate for each grade. Of course, most eighth and ninth graders have more cognitive ability than fifth and sixth graders, so teachers should take care to make sure that the activity is developmentally appropriate for the particular grade.

Activities for introducing the concept of each step begin each chapter and can be used with grades five through nine, with or without modification. Included also are additional strategies for increasing students' skill base for each step—a "bag of tricks" from which they can consult for various information searching needs. Each of the Big6 chapters contains a chart for specific technology applications. For the sake of the activities, "teacher" refers to whoever is conducting the instruction, whether it is the classroom or subject-area teacher, library media specialist, or technology teacher.

If students have not had any experience with Big6, you may want to introduce the process by taking the students through each step using as an example, the purchase of an MP3 player or other popular gadget. For curricular assignments and projects, introduce each Big6 step to students by displaying all the steps so that students can place in context the specific step on which the class is working. Teachers may also want to write the specific instructions for each step for the current assignment directly on the projected Big6 display. Students can easily understand that, from one assignment to the next, the steps remain the same while the content changes. The transferability of the process becomes very apparent.

Chapter Twelve puts it all together with complete units of instruction with a focus on typical middle school subjects, including grades five and nine. This final chapter shows how to correlate the Big6 Skills with the state's prescribed curriculum and tested skills. It also illustrates how to apply strategies to the curriculum and offers several complete units (English language arts, math, social studies, and science) within the Big6 framework. Teachers may use the instructional units as models to design lessons for their curriculum needs or modify the lessons to reflect their specific state's curriculum standards for that subject area and grade level. Chapter Twelve also guides library media specialists and teachers in developing useful pathfinders for individual units of instruction.

Chapter 6

Task Definition

D esigning a good task is the key to a successful information search. A meaningful and developmentally appropriate task will motivate your students to engage in the content. Think of designing and delivering a good task as a multistep process for you and your students: identifying content and skills objectives, creating an engaging information problem, defining a specific task, and determining the information needed to solve the problem.

Get Started

Introduce Task Definition to Students: Plan

Identify the Content Objectives in Which Students Will Engage
Closely align the content objectives to the state or school curriculum standards.

Example: Seventh Grade State Government

The student understands the basic principles reflected in the state constitution. The student is expected to:

(A) Identify how the state constitution reflects the principles of limited government, checks and balances, federalism, separation of powers, popular sovereignty, and individual rights; and

(B) Identify the influence of ideas from the U.S. Constitution on the state constitution.

The student understands the structure and functions of government created by the state constitution. The student is expected to:

(A) Describe the structure and functions of government at municipal, county, and state levels;

(B) Identify major sources of revenue for state and local governments; and

(C) Describe the structure and governance of state public education.

(Modified from the Texas Essential Knowledge and Skills for seventh grade social studies <http://www.tea.state.tx.us/rules/tac/chapter113/ch113b.html#113.23>.)

Big6 #1.1: Define the Problem—Create an Information Problem Based on the Content Objectives

An information problem will ensure that students will *want to* and *need to* engage in the content in order to solve the problem. Even though this step seems complicated and optional, it goes a long way toward placing the content in a context that has meaning to the student. This also sets the stage for using the Big6 process. The information problem must be cognitively appropriate for the learner. While the problem may be whimsical or merely motivational, you can also design an authentic problem—one that students may encounter now or in the future—to give the content meaning. Any grade level's content curriculum can be turned into an information problem.

Example: You work for the (imaginary) Office for Immigrant Education whose purpose is to teach immigrants about the state, county, and city government. The office informs immigrants about their state and local governments so they have the option to participate and make informed decisions for themselves and their families. Immigrants will attend several classes to learn about government. Your classmates will field test the lesson and activity your group develops. What do you need to do? Or, in other words, what is your task? (See this chapter for additional examples of information problems from other subject areas.)

Higher-Level Thinking Considerations with Task Definition and Content Objectives

Merely using the Big6 process as a means for acquiring content and presenting results will not ensure that students are exercising in higher-level thought throughout the information search process. Evidence of higher-level thinking—application, analysis, synthesis, and evaluation—is typically found in the Synthesis step of the Big6, both in #5.1 and #5.2 (Bloom, 1956). However, most students will think on a higher level if the task requires more than a copy-and-paste effort. The teacher must write the higher-level requirements into the task, in addition to having students provide evidence of higher-level thought in the Synthesis step. In Task Definition, prepare students for the higher level of thought the final product will require. Set expectations high, build them into the task, and watch and be amazed with your students' brilliant efforts!

Big6 #1.2: Identify the Information Needed—Decide What Information the Students Need to Have in Order to Do the Task

Many information problems, such as the one above, lend themselves to dividing the class into groups. Decide how you will group the class, then develop questions that students in each group will need to know in order to successfully complete the task. Why should you write the information needed in question form?

1. The information needed is presented clearly, without much confusion about its meaning.

2. By middle school, students are accustomed to finding "answers" to "questions."

3. It is easy to say, for Information Seeking Strategies, "Which sources can help us answer our questions?"

4. When helping a student use a source for information, you can easily say "The answer to that question is on this page. Can you find it?"

Include higher-order questions, along with knowledge and comprehension, to make the information search more than a copy-and-paste activity. The questions for the group studying the state constitution may look like this:

1. How does the state constitution reflect the principles of limited government?

2. How does the state constitution limit government power through checks and balances?

3. What is federalism? What does it have to do with the state constitution?

4. What is "separation of powers?" Why is it important?

5. What is "popular sovereignty?" Why is it important?

6. What are some individual rights the people of our state have?

7. What rights do immigrants have? Why are these rights important to immigrants?

8. How might immigrants use information about the state constitution?

9. What is your opinion about the state constitution using "Almighty God" in the Bill of Rights? Do you think this means all deities or just the Christian God? Do you think the wording should be changed?

Other groups for the above set of objectives may include: (1) structure and functions of municipal government, including major sources of revenue; (2) structure and function of county government, including major sources of revenue; (3) structure and function of state government, including major sources of revenue; and (4) structure and governance of state public education. You would develop questions for each of these groups accordingly.

Deliver Instruction

Big6 #1.1: Define the Problem—Present the Information Problem to the Class

Discuss the information problem so that the class fully understands it before asking, "What is your task?" Traditionally, instead of asking students to figure out their task, teachers tell students exactly what they need to do in order to accomplish the step. Teachers usually discuss the final product at this time. While the strategy may prove successful, it does not give students an opportunity to think for themselves. In their adolescent and adult lives, there are many occasions—most outside of the academic setting—where students will need to determine what needs to be done in order to solve a problem. Provide opportunities for students to practice solving problems, and the goal of becoming a life-long learner is within reach.

Guide Students in Brainstorming the Task

In small groups (not necessarily the ones in which they will continue to work), have students discuss the nature of the task and what the class will need to do in order to complete the task. Call on each group to present its ideas from the brainstorming session as you record and project each. After recording all ideas, students may not completely understand the task, so you may need to summarize. For example, "So in other words, what we need to do is *learn about the state constitution and forms of state and local government and then present each concept in some way so that the immigrants in our imaginary classes can understand it.* We can use the Big6 to do this. We just accomplished Big6 #1.1: Define the Problem."

Show a poster of the Big6 or project the six steps, reading each step (if the class is not familiar with the process), while emphasizing Task Definition. Show students that each step has two parts and they just completed the first part of Task Definition: #1.1 Define the Problem. Record the task on the displayed Big6 chart in the appropriate place. Tell students that they will now help complete step#1.2: Identify the Information Needed.

Big6 #1.2: Identify the Information Needed—Students Generate a List of Information Questions

Certainly, the teacher can and does give the class (or groups) the list of questions that they will need to research. However, providing students with the opportunity to list what they need to and want to know will give them ownership in the content and motivate them to locate and use information. It will also provide meaningful and valuable practice for a critical information skill.

When you divide the class into its working groups (see section in this chapter for ideas about grouping), have each group brainstorm a list of questions it will need to research in order to do the task. After all groups have exhausted their ideas, provide them with your list and ask them to add any questions they missed to the end of their list. The more often students brainstorm needed questions and interact with your questions, the more they will gain proficiency in writing their own.

After you give students your list of questions to add to their own, tell them that they may not find "answers" to some of the questions (higher order), but will need to keep the higher-order questions in mind as they find answers to the knowledge-level questions. They will be expected to give thoughtful responses to the higher-level questions in the Synthesis step of the Big6 process.

Highlight the questions in which students can locate "answers." Divide these questions so that each student has a subset for which he or she is responsible. Have each student write his or her questions on a note taking organizer. Two types of organizers you may consider are the data chart and note taking form, both found in Chapter Nine.

Discuss and Assign the Final Product

An optional step, but fitting nicely at this point of the Task Definition, is discussing Big6 #5: Synthesis. Students should understand that the task will result in a meaningful product. The product can be assigned by the teacher (most typical arrangement) or may be chosen by the students. If the task results in an obvious product, such as a museum display for the science example below, it is difficult to separate the task from its result. However, most tasks need not result in a specific creation. No matter how students will display their results, it is logical to discuss the final product with the task. This will also help motivate students to continue the process. See Chapter Ten for details in Synthesis.

Additional Examples of Information Problems from Other Subject Areas

Science (Rock Cycle)

1. Present the problem to the class: The Museum of Natural History has many elementary-age students visiting its rocks and minerals displays. The young students are unable to understand the significance of the rock cycle. Pretend that the museum has come to the class for help since this is one area that we study. What could we do?

2. In groups, the students should brainstorm solutions to the problem.

3. On the projector or white board, list the students' solutions. The first few times, the students will most likely list products as the solution to the problem (such as make a booklet about the rock cycle to send home with young students or construct a PowerPoint slide show for the museum computer).

4. Summarize their solutions: "What you are saying is . . . to solve this problem, we first need to learn about the rock cycle in order to present information about it to younger children. We could present the information in one of the ways you suggested."

5. Tell students that they will use the Big6 to solve the problem and that they have already completed the first part of the process. For Big6 #1.1, write "Learn about the _____." In this case it would be: "Learn about the rock cycle and present it to young children for the museum's display."

Regions of the state: Our school has a diverse student population. New students do not know anything about the state. Our class studies the state in social studies. What can we do to help new students know about the state?

Basketball skills and rules: All of your friends are playing basketball. You don't know the rules, but want to join in the game. What is your task?

Botany: You are planning a garden. Which plants will do best? How will understanding the structure of plants help you decide? What is your task?

Solar system: You work for NASA. You are the commander of the Pathfinder II that will carry astronauts to Mars (or another planet). You must prepare your crew for the trip. What is your task?

Civil War: Your city council wishes to create a museum of the Civil War using artifacts that symbolize the war. They also want to feature the area's contribution to the war effort. What is your task?

Graphing and other math skills: The student council wants to sell snacks in the cafeteria during lunch to earn money for community service projects. It has come to us for help in determining which snacks will sell the best and at the least cost to them. What is our task?

Women's History Month: Imagine that the U.S. Postal Service wants to add a series of stamps on America's outstanding women. They want the public's suggestions on women to include. What is the task?

Astronomy (explain how life on earth is affected by its unique placement and orientation in our solar system): Earth is becoming overpopulated in the 21st century. Your NASA research team must determine if other planets are habitable. What is your task?

Recycling: Students are throwing away too many paper products. How can we help students understand which materials to put in the recycle bin and which to throw away? What is our task?

Art (color): You have been commissioned to paint murals in a children's hospital waiting room and other public areas. The board of directors wants murals with warm or cool colors depending on the function of the room. What is your task?

Music (learning names of notes): Young children have a difficult time remembering the names of the notes. How can we help young children learn the names of notes and their corresponding keys on the keyboard? What is your task?

Fail-safe strategies for any subject content: Giving students a reason to teach younger students or to present their findings to their peers works for any content. Tell your students that a younger class is interested in (subject content) and does not have materials that they can understand about (subject content) and need the help of our class because we study that subject. What can we do to help? Or, talk about the textbook's publisher having to condense the content to fit on a page or in several paragraphs due to space restraints. Tell the class how interesting the content is and how much is left out of the textbook. What can we do to learn more than the text is presenting? You can have groups of students become "experts" in subtopics and present to one another.

Additional Strategies for Engaging Students in Task Definition

Show the Importance of the Task

Students need to understand that comprehension of the task is critical for success. This quick activity can do the trick. Complete the activity the day after you introduce the task. It can even be accomplished after the class completes Big6 #1.2—identifying the information needed to do the task.

1. Each student writes the task in his or her own words.
2. Read aloud and compare to others in the class (without commenting on others' interpretations).
3. The teacher checks for understanding by restating and displaying the task as summarized the day before.
4. Tell students to compare their interpretation to that which is displayed. Could they do this successfully as an independent assignment?
5. Have each student record the correct task. Tell them that knowing what to do is the first step toward success.

Develop Common Questions

Many times, the subject requires that students find out the same information about different topics within a unit. For example, a seventh grade class may be studying biographies about notable state leaders. The teacher knows that while each student or group of students is studying a different person, they will need the same basic information about each. Instead of the teacher telling the students the information to find, students can participate in an activity to generate the list of questions (with the teacher's final approval, of course). This strategy gives students the responsibility for determining what information is important to know. The teacher can help with the appropriate wording for questions, and has the option to add more questions if needed.

Students in groups will brainstorm a list of questions that they need to research about their topic. For example, a sixth grade class is studying the world's explorers. One group brainstorms a list of questions about Christopher Columbus as another group lists questions about Vasco de Gama. Once all groups are finished brainstorming and their questions are displayed on large chart paper for all to see, have the groups walk around to read each list, finding those questions that are similar in content to their own. The teacher can place the pages around the room and set a timer for groups to rotate from page to page. Have the class discuss which questions are similar on each group's list. The teacher will write common questions on the display, rewording them as needed (because groups may use various phrases to mean the same thing), and make a list of several questions that all students will use for Big6 #1.2. The teacher can add questions to the list that she knows will be important to the research. Students may also find information that will be unique to their topic as they engage in the note taking process in Big6 #4: Use of Information.

Identify Keywords

Even though students will usually use keywords during Location and Access, consider having them generate at least a partial list during the Task Definition phase. The following steps will help your students identify important keywords and related words, aiding them in using subscription databases, the online library catalog, search engines, indices, tables of content, and in accessing the information on a page. You may want to model these steps for the class.

Ask students to look at the questions they created for Big6 #1.2, including those you provided. Each student should underline the important keywords (those words that help "unlock" the meaning of the sentence) in each question. On the same paper, write related words and phrases for each keyword. Using colored pencils or ink will separate the original question from the related words. Students should be allowed to help each other or use a thesaurus to generate as many related words as possible. The teacher may also suggest related words. Tell students that these words will help them later when they are trying to find and use information from sources, as the words used in the source may vary slightly from those in the original question.

Example:

What <u>rights</u> do <u>immigrants</u> have? (underline keywords)
Rights=privileges, civil rights, civil liberties, liberties, human rights
Immigrant=émigré, migrant, refugee, alien (write related words in contrasting color)

Keyword Builder

Drawing a graphic organizer will help students understand the hierarchy of creating keywords. Figure 6.1 illustrates using a pencil and paper, Inspiration™ Software, concept-mapping freeware Cmap <http://cmap.ihmc.us>, or drawing tools in a word processor to create the organizer.

Figure 6.1: Keyword Builder

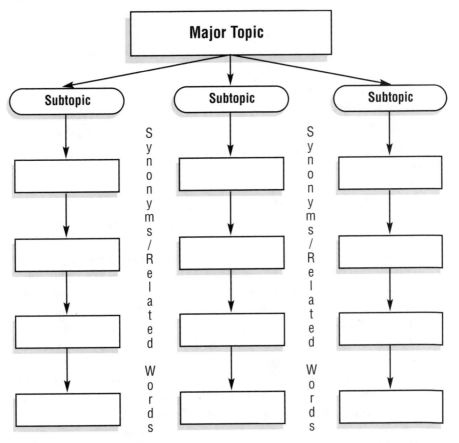

Eisenberg, Michael B. and Berkowitz, Robert E. Information Problem-Solving: The Big Six Skills Approach to Library & information Skills Instruction. *Norwood, NJ: Ablex Publishing Company, 1990, p. 119.*
Formatted by Barbara A. Jansen, 2002.

Group Work

When employees know how to function in a group they gain an advantage in the workplace. Teachers need to provide many opportunities for group collaboration, and the information search process allows for working in a group in meaningful ways. Of course, not all topics lend themselves to grouping students, but most do. Groups should consist of two to four students (there is such a thing as the fifth wheel!). Consider putting students in groups when you are first introducing Big6 to the class so that they can collaborate and share experiences in learning the new process and strategies. Working in groups includes these benefits:

a. Reducing the time it takes to gather information.

b. Sharing work responsibilities, giving students more time for in-depth research.

c. Creating dependence among group members, which raises their level of concern and commitment.

d. Allowing teachers to grade individual participation and note taking efforts.

e. Combining brain power—several brains are usually more creative and efficient than one.

f. Learning to work with others—an important skill in most jobs.

g. Choosing not to cooperate with the group, a student can do the entire project alone—although this rarely happens.

Individual Student-Selected Topics

Often, the curriculum requires that students complete an individual research project: history fair, science fair, or research paper for health or literature, for example. Guide students in their topic selection by encouraging them to explore their own interests and by having students use available technologies for choosing topics (see below for technology ideas for topic selection).

Direct students to think about topics that interest them, then connect that interest to the requirements of the assignment. For example, if the history fair has a broad topic such as "Change over time in U.S. History" (typical eighth grade curriculum) and the student is passionate about cars, consider connecting the topics in this way: "To what extent has the design of automobiles over time influenced the way Americans buy and use their cars?" Here is another example for a student who loves photography: "How has photography and its advances changed the way Americans use their cameras for leisure?"

Helping students who have no ideas for a topic or have no definite interest is more of a challenge. Students can browse the library shelves in the appropriate section or use the browse feature for the online databases to which the school has subscriptions, as well as subject directories on the free Web, such as KidsClick <http://www.kidsclick.org>. Or, students can use an idea generator such as the one in Figure 6.2. The guide helps students choose one topic from several topics in which they may be interested.

Figure 6.2: Idea Generator

Idea Generator for Selecting a Topic		
Directions	**Example**	**Your ideas**
1. Write the subject here. For example: Civil War, health, science fair, history fair, culture fair, state history	Science fair	
2. List five things about the subject that you think are interesting.	1. Armadillos 2. Wild flowers 3. Earthquakes 4. Dogs 5. Trans fats	1. 2. 3. 4. 5.
3. Of the five things you listed, which one would you choose if you could study only one thing the rest of the year?	Dogs	
4. List five things about your topic that you find interesting. You can write this list in question form to make this step easier.	1. Why do some dogs bark so much more than others? 2. Why do dogs seem friendlier than cats? 3. How much do dogs sleep? 4. Does my dog have preferences for dog food? 5. My aunt got two 5-year-old dogs that were only used for breeding. Why don't they play?	1. 2. 3. 4. 5.
5. Which one of the above list would you choose if you could only study one thing for the rest the year?	Why do dogs seem friendlier than cats?	
6. Will the topic you chose work for the assignment? (Ask your teacher.) If yes, then keep it. If no, then choose another from number 4 or go back to number 3.	Yes or no (underline one) If no, write new topic here: Does my dog have preferences for dog food?	Yes or no (underline one) If no, write new topic here:
7. Have your teacher look at your topic and help you revise it if needed. Write your revised topic here.	Do different breeds of dogs prefer one type of dog food over another?	

Use a Wiki to Organize and Present a Big6 Project

"A wiki is a type of Web site that allows users to easily add and edit content and is especially suited for collaborative writing" (Wiki). Create a wiki for your Big6 curriculum project; it is easy and free using a service such as David Weekly's Peanut Butter Wiki <http://www.pbwiki.com>. If your district or school cannot host your class project pages or will not allow students to post pages, you and your students can create and edit your own wikis. Wiki editing is much easier than coding hypertext mark up language (HTML) or using Web authoring software. You can use a project wiki to introduce the unit and each step of the Big6 as your students create and collaborate using group wikis to maintain interest and stay organized. You can also upload documents students will need for the project, putting an end to students losing important assignment sheets.

On your wiki home page (the project wiki), you will introduce the project (Figure 6.1). The home page is a good place to write the information problem that will get students interested and motivated to want to study the content. Once you put students in groups for the subtopics, have each group create a wiki (you assign the password or record the one they give you). Instruct groups to create a sidebar listing each of the Big6 Steps. As you instruct students in the specifics of each step, each group will add a page, including ideas and responses to assignments. See below for Task Definition, and subsequent chapters for strategies.

Group wiki home page: On the group's home page, students can put their names and the topic they are studying. Have them paste the project URL on their home page. They can also copy and paste the information problem on the page.

Figure 6.3 Project Wiki: Introductory Page

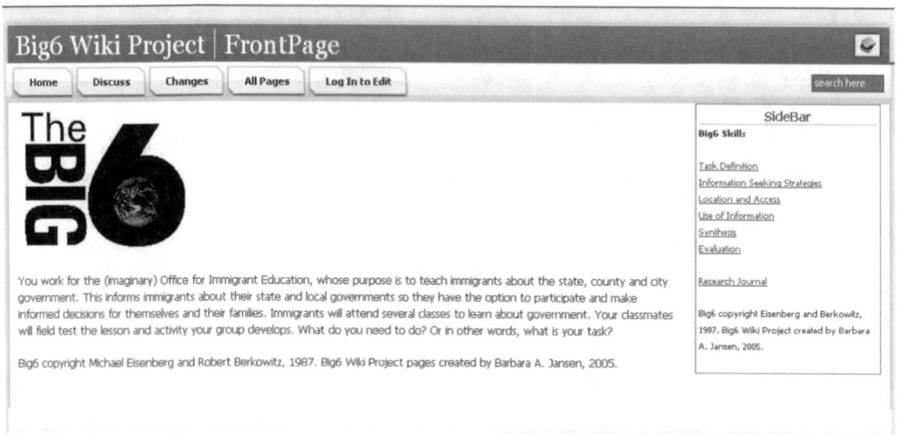

Wiki Task Definition Page

Project wiki: Define the task for the students on the project wiki's Task Definition page (Figure 6.4), including content questions that students will research in order to satisfy the task.

Group wikis: In addition, each group writes on its own Task Definition page with the task as detailed by the teacher and the project wiki. You may want students to write the task in their own words. Students will include the project wiki's uniform resource locator (URL) on their task definition page or home page so it is easily accessible. Each group must supply you with its password or you can assign the password that everyone will use. Students can make up a group name based on their topic.

On the group's Task Definition pages, each can write its own questions for Big6 #1.2 of the task (What information do we need?). The group can then copy and paste the questions posted on the project wiki to add to their list. The questions posted on the project wiki's Task Definition page will be those that satisfy the content requirements.

Figure 6.4: Project Wiki: Task Definition

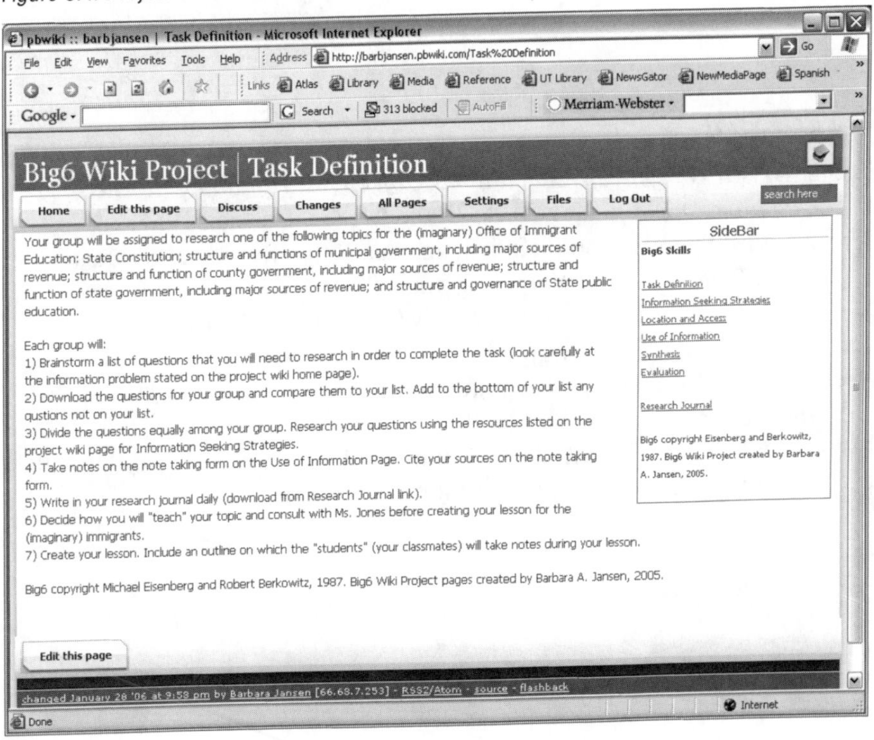

Specific Uses of Technology

Figure 6.5: Possible Uses of Technology for Task Definition

Task Definition 1.1 Define the task	Possible technologies used *Class project:* Use a wiki to organize the class project and group wikis for members of groups to collaborate on the project. *Self-selected topics:* electronic databases (many allow browsing), online library catalog, browsing electronic subject directories such as Yahooligans™ <http://www.yahooligans.com> or KidsClick <http://www.kidsclick.org>
1.2 Identify the information needed	*Developing a list of information needed:* Brainstorming software such as Inspiration™ Software, word processing. Collaborating with other classes and Schools to identify information needed: e-mail, word-processed attachments, chat or instant messaging, electronic bulletin or discussion boards, wikis, or blogs (with care)

Works Cited

Bloom, B. S. *Taxonomy of Educational Objectives, Handbook I: The Cognitive Domain.* New York: David McKay Co Inc., 1956.

"Chapter 113. State Essential Knowledge and Skills for Social Studies." 1998. *State Essential Knowledge and Skills (TEKS).* State Education Agency. 05 June 2004 <http://www.tea.state.tx.us/rules/tac/chapter113/ch113b.html#113.23>.

Weekly, David. "Re: permission requested." E-mail to Barbara Jansen. 03 January 06.

"Wiki." *Wikipedia.* 27 Nov. 2001. Wikimedia Foundation, Inc. 28 Jan. 2006 <http://en.wikipedia.org/wiki/Wiki>.

The BIG 6

Chapter 7

Information Seeking Strategies

TexasIndians.com <http://www.texasindians.com> and Crystalinks.com/egyptafterlife.html <http://www.crystalinks.com/egyptafterlife.html>: What do these two Web sites have in common? They are two popular sites students use in school projects about Native Americans and ancient Egypt. They are not authoritative and one must question their accuracy, yet many teachers accept them as valid sources of information. Upon close inspection, we find that one is authored by a gentleman who posts no credentials, does not cite his sources, and asks children to send him money for his work. Another, posted by a woman whose site appears valid, contains no in-text citation or bibliography, and consists of huge sections of text identical to that found in Encyclopædia Britannica Online. Not only that, she claims to be a psychic who has been visited by aliens!

Once upon a time, before the Internet, school libraries housed the main sources of information for school papers and projects. Before finding its way onto the shelf, each book, magazine, or video went through a rigid editing process, after which the librarian carefully selected the source for the collection based on positive reviews, the reputation of the publisher or author, and the item's relevance to the curriculum. Students did not need to evaluate sources for accuracy and authority, only judge for relevancy for their particular personal or academic need. Now that the Internet is so widely available in our schools and homes, it is imperative that we give our middle school children an awareness that sites found on the free Web must be evaluated for accuracy and authority, in addition to a set of skills allowing them to perform these evaluations. Unless we guide them otherwise, students think Google <http://www.google.com> or Yahoo <http://www.yahoo.com> are their one-stop source of information. And, as importantly, we need to guide children to reputable sources of information on library shelves and in those electronic databases to which your school subscribes. You will find detailed information about Web site evaluation in this chapter.

Library media specialists will want to introduce students to resources available through the library (books, periodicals, audiovisual materials, and subscription databases) and to those on the free Web. Typically this will occur through direct instruction during the second step of the Big6 process—Information Seeking Strategies—as library media specialists collaborate with teachers to integrate these sources into the subject area curricula. Of course, students can help brainstorm an initial list, but the librarian will use his judgment to narrow the list to the best sources, adding additional sources as needed.

Get Started

Big6 #2.1: Determine All Possible Sources—Introduce Information Seeking Strategies to Students: Plan

The library media specialist, alongside the teacher, examines the information students will need to locate in order to satisfy the requirements set forth in Task Definition. She decides in which resources students will find the "answers" and works with the classroom teacher to determine if students have the reading proficiency required to successfully engage in the sources. If some students read below the level of the source, the special education or reading specialist may be able to modify sources or provide additional strategies or materials for these students.

Once appropriate materials are identified, the teaching team needs to decide how students will engage in Big6 #2: Information Seeking Strategies #2.1: Brainstorm All Possible Sources, and #2.2: Select Best Sources. Occasionally, you will want to tell students (especially in fifth and sixth grades) which sources they will use. Often, you will guide students to appropriate sources. Either way, students should have opportunities to suggest relevant sources during a brainstorming session as often as possible to give them experience and expertise in selecting best sources. The activity below will jump-start students in brainstorming sources.

Deliver Instruction

Big6 #2.1: Determine All Possible Sources and 2.2: Select the Best Sources

Even though you already know which sources of information students will most likely use, getting students to brainstorm a list helps them gain an awareness of the scope of sources and allows the library media specialist or teacher to discuss each source suggested by students. Display the Big6 chart and direct students' attention to Big6 #2: Information Seeking Strategies, and its subskill #2.1: Brainstorming Possible Sources. The activity presented below will facilitate the brainstorming process:

Process of Exclusion—Brainstorming Sources of Information

1. Cut notebook paper in half lengthwise and give a piece to each group of students.

2. Each group brainstorms and records possible sources that will contain answers to its questions. Suggest that students consider those found on library shelves as well as online and in person.

3. The teacher uses the "Process of Exclusion" to record each group's list.

   a. The first group reads its entire list as the teacher records and displays the sources.

   b. Instruct the other groups to check off any of these resources that appear on their lists.

   c. The second group reads only those items that do not have a checkmark while other groups place checkmarks by those items on their list that the second group reads.

   d. Continue until all groups have read items that have no checkmarks.

   e. The instructor adds any resources to the list that the groups missed and resources that he wants to introduce to the class.

4. Discuss the benefits and drawbacks of each source. Those not available or that will not meet the requirements of the task should be crossed off the list. Most likely students will have "Internet" or "Google" on their lists. Instead, tell students that they need Web sites that contain content about their topic. Discuss with the students that the Internet and search engines are not actual sources, but ways of accessing content-related Web sites; therefore, Big6 #3: Location and Access will be the step that helps them use the Internet and Google.

5. The teacher instructs each group to choose two to four sources from the displayed list that will best meet the needs of the task. (They may need to do this for each question being answered in the task, as not all resources will answer all questions.) Instruct each group to read aloud which ones it has chosen. Place checkmarks beside each resource on the displayed list as it is chosen. The ones with the most checkmarks will most likely be the resources that the class will use for that assignment. The instructor may direct groups to include particular sources—especially if he is introducing a new or unknown resource to the class. Consider allowing individual groups to add resources of their own with your approval.

6. Direct students' attention to the displayed Big6 chart or poster. Tell them that they have completed both parts of Big6 #2: Information Seeking Strategies—

2.1: Brainstorm all Possible Sources and #2.2 Select Best Sources. Students can record the sources in a research notebook or on a Big6 chart.

The benefits of using the "Process of Exclusion" to introduce step two of the process to students include (1) requiring students to listen to each other to avoid repetition when sharing results of brainstorming; (2) allowing the instructor to introduce new or previously unknown resources to students; (3) helping the instructor determine which skills she needs to teach in order for students to access and use general or specific sources; and (4) giving students a focus for engaging in the assignment—they have a place to start and various resources to consult if the computer stations are in use.

Additional Strategies for Engaging Students in Information Seeking Strategies

Determine Types of Information Needed

Questions identified in Task Definition #1.2 require that students search for a particular type of information. For example, if a student is researching the question "What is federalism?" she needs to find a definition or an explanation. The question "What is the atmospheric make-up of Venus?" requires searching for facts, and "How did Susan B. Anthony affect women today?" needs biographical information. Teaching children how to identify the types of information imbedded in their research questions will help them make the distinction among the resources they will choose.

Create a table such as the one in Figure 7.1. Assist students in completing it to help them identify the types of information they need for specific questions.

Figure 7.1: Identifying Types of Information

Question (Write the questions for which you are responsible for researching.)	Type of Information Needed (General, factual, overview, background statistics, explanations; definitions; specific, in depth; primary sources, first-person accounts; controversial issues, pro and con; images, audio, video, animations; maps; biographical; news and current events)
Example: "What did Susan B. Anthony do that affected women of today?"	Biographical
Example: "What rights do women have today that they did not have in 1890?"	

The next step identifies the resources that deliver the needed information type.

Figure 7.2: Chart for Identifying the Best Sources for Specific Types of Information

What type of information do I need?	Which library resources and subscription databases may deliver the information I need? (List here those available through your library—examples provided for subscription databases)	What other sources can I use? (Find URLs of example sites in Works Cited section at the end of this chapter)
General, factual, overview, background, statistics, explanations	Encyclopedias and other reference books: Include encyclopedia titles available on the shelf in the library and books such as World Almanac, Information Please, Guiness Book of World Records. Online encyclopedias and other encyclopedic sources: Include those to which your library subscribes or has access (through region or state-funded initiatives) such as Compton's by Britannica, World Book Online, and Gale Junior Reference Collection Topic Overviews, eLibrary Reference, EBSCO Middle Search Plus Reference Books, and SIRS Discoverer.	Free Web sites: List here those free encyclopedias that you will allow students to use, including statistical data such as CIA World Fact Book and Infoplease.
Definitions, including foreign language	Dictionaries: Include those you have available on the library shelves, including foreign language. Online dictionaries available through subscription: Include those you have available through subscription such as Merriam-Webster Unabridged Online.	Free Web sites: Approved dictionaries
Specific, in depth	Books in nonfiction section of the library and subject-specific encyclopedias. Subscription databases such as EBSCO Host History Reference Center, Gale Junior Reference Collection.	Free Web sites: Include here those subject–specific sites selected by teachers and librarians. Experts: University professors, business executives, lawyers, doctors, accountants, directors of nonprofit agencies, service professionals: police, nurses, city government.
Primary sources, first person accounts	Library books: Include titles containing primary sources. Subscription databases: Include those titles that contain primary sources such as EBSCO Middle Search Plus and Student Research Center (not many databases targeted to middle schools contain primary sources such as EBSCO Middle Search Plus and Student Research Center. (Not many databases targeted to middle schools contain primary source materials. Access to high school databases will provide more documents.)	Free Web sites: Include approved sites such as Library of Congress American Memory Collection.

Controversial issues, pro and con	Library books: Some middle school libraries may have limited nonfiction books that cover specific controversial topics. Develop the collection for these topics, if indeed they are covered in the curriculum. Encourage middle school students to borrow from the high school or public library if needed and allowed in your district. Subscription databases: All elementary and middle schools subscription databases will have articles on controversial topics. Students will need to read carefully to see if a slant is presented. High school databases such as Gale Opposing View Points Resource Center and SIRS Researcher have articles obviously for or against.	Free Web sites selected for their authority on controversial issues. Experts in the field of study, journalists, lay people (for opinions.)
Images, audio, video, animations	Consider making video and DVD in library collections available to students for specific needs. Subscription databases: Most include images, some include audio and video including EBSCO Middle Search Plus, ProQuest eLibrary, and Gale Junior Reference Collection.	Free Web sites: Choose authoritative and accurate sources for student access.
Maps	Library atlases: List those held by your library. Subscription databases: Those in your holdings such as Britannica Online World Atlas, eLibrary, and others.	Free Web sites: Select authoritative sites such as the Atlapedia and Map Machine.
Biographies	Library books Subscription databases: All middle school databases contain biographical material.	Free Web sites: Include approved sources of biographies for the specific subject researched.
News and current events	Library magazine and newspaper collections Subscription databases: General databases such as EBSCO Middle Search, Newsbank Kids, SIRS Discoverer, Gale Junior Reference Collection, and eLibrary all contain news and current events.	Free Web sites: Select sources such as local and national news station and newspaper sites.
Peer reviewed, scholarly	Subscription databases: eLibrary (check peer-reviewed), Middle Search (check peer-reviewed)	TV and radio

Identify the Best Sources for Specific Types of Information

Teachers often think about format such as print, nonprint, and electronic sources. Help students first think about the type of information needed, then choose the best source no matter the format. Middle school students may not understand "print" formats as teachers and library media specialists think of them (books, periodicals, and reference books that are bound and available on the library or bookstore shelves). These formats are also available electronically and (most) can be printed to paper, so this distinction may not make sense to grade school children.

Figure 7.2 consists of information types needed for typical curricular units of instruction in grades five through nine. In guiding children to resources, they will answer three questions: What type of information do I need? Which library resources and subscription databases may contain the information I need? What other sources can I use?

The library media specialist may choose to make a similar chart to post in the library, labs, classrooms, and on the school library's Web site.

Demonstrate Subscription Services That Contain Multiple Databases

Middle school students and even those in high school have a difficult time discerning between the subscription services, the individual databases in the collection, and the multiple titles stored in a single database. If your library holds a subscription to a service such as EBSCOHost®, Thomson Gale™, ProQuest® K-12, or SIRS®, show students the hierarchy of the collections to help them understand the vast amount and type of information contained in a single service. Use a diagram similar to the one in Figure 7.3, as well as demonstrate the hierarchy of holdings contained in the service, so students understand the concept. You will need to direct middle school students to the appropriate databases within the service. Recently, subscription services allow students to easily search multiple databases, such as EBSCO's Student Research Center® and Thomson Gale's Power Search.

Figure 7.3 Example of Hierarchy of Subscription Services

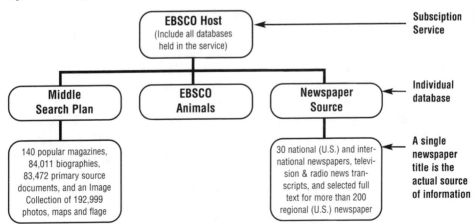

Determine Content of Subscription Services and Databases

Each database may contain one or more sources, and knowing what type of information is included will help educators choose appropriate databases for particular information needs. ProQuest's eLibrary®, SIRS Discoverer®, EBSCO Student Research Center, EBSCO Middle Search Plus®, and EBSCO Kids Search® all allow the user to select specific formats of information, such as graphics, reference books, magazines, or audio. Some databases contain only periodicals such as Newsbank™, EBSCO's Middle Search Plus, and Thomson Gale's Junior Edition. In addition, most databases feature a directory of subjects allowing students to browse categories.

Web Sites Included within Subscription Databases

Some online subscription databases and encyclopedias include links to sites available on the free Web. Editors or indexers carefully choose these sites for inclusion in the subscription databases by evaluating the criteria such as relevance, authority, age appropriateness, and accuracy. Possibly containing some advertising, these sites offer information that may extend that in the database. These sites typically open in a new window, but take students out of the protected database. The careful educator will preview these sites before allowing student access. You will need to decide whether or not you want your students to use the free Web sites and instruct them accordingly.

Evaluate Free Web Sites for Accuracy and Authority

With the privilege of finding sites on the free Web comes the responsibility of evaluating them. If educators allow students to search for and use sites found on the free Web, they must require students to formally evaluate these sites for accuracy and authority, turning in the evaluations with their final products. If students are not required to evaluate sites found on the free Web, they should at least have to get permission to use individual sites in assignments and projects. Instructing students in Web evaluation remains one of the most important responsibilities of teachers and library media specialists. Fifth and sixth graders probably do not have the cognitive skills required to determine if a Web site is accurate and authoritative. Identifying authorship on many Web sites proves difficult even for some educators. In addition, Web searching is time-consuming and returns up to several million sites. Consider requiring young learners to use those sites provided through subscription services such as netTrekker® <http://www.nettrekker.com> or WebFeet™ <http://www.webfeetguides.com> (now owned by Thomson Gale), subscription databases, and those sites chosen by the teacher and librarian. However, good practice may dictate that we at least introduce Web evaluation to young learners, making them aware of its need and the process by which we evaluate Web sites for their use.

Web Evaluation for Young Learners in Grades Five and Six

Diane Lauer's "Five Ws of Web Site Evaluation" <http://www.dianelauer.com/fivewww/webeval.html> presents the basic concepts of Web evaluation. The 5Ws include: Who, What, Where, When, and Why.

The 5Ws of Web Evaluation

Who wrote the pages and are they an expert in the field?

- Can you tell who the author is? If not, what organization is sponsoring this Web site?
- Is the author/sponsor well-regarded in this field?
- Is there a place on the Web site where you can contact the author/sponsor?
- Are you led to additional information about the author? A place of work? Biographical info?
- How did you get here? Did you link to this site from a site you trust?

What is the purpose of the site?

- Is this page mostly fact or mostly opinion?
- Does the author attempt to over-generalize or simplify information as to detract from fact?
- Do any of the facts appear out of context? Are they applied in a way to persuade you?
- Are there links to the organization sponsoring the page? Or, does this seem like a lone person trying to voice his/her opinion?
- Is the page actually an advertisement disguised as information?

Where does the information come from?

- Does the author let the reader know where the information came from? Did he/she provide citations?
- Do the citations appear to be accurate and valid?
- Can you double-check the citations because the author linked to them?
- Does the author provide links to related Web sites you can use to continue your research?

When was the site created, updated, or last worked on?

- Does the date this Web site was created appear on it somewhere?
- Can you tell when this information was last updated?
- If not, can you tell how old the information is by the language used in the writing? The citations?
- Does it matter to you whether this information is outdated? Why?

Demonstrate to the class how you would use the 5 Ws to evaluate a Web site. Choose two Web sites: one whose authority is simply stated and one with questionable or no author. Discuss each component and connect it to each Web site. If you want the class to practice evaluating Web sites, divide the class into groups of two or three and assign each group the same Web site for evaluation. Have each group discuss and identify in the Web site each component of the 5 Ws. Or, if time is limited, divide the class into five groups and have each identify a different component (who, what, where, when, or why) of the Web site. Create a simple worksheet for students to record their findings. Have a second, more challenging site to give to those groups who finish quickly. When all groups are finished, go over each of the 5 Ws and discuss the children's findings.

Web Evaluation for Grades Seven, Eight, and Nine

Whether or not we allow the use of free Web sites in assignments, students are searching the free Web for a variety of reasons. Mostly, they may be looking for products or games, but often young people seek information of a sensitive, personal nature, depending on the Web to maintain privacy. While 12 to 15-year-old children will not evaluate sites they seek for personal need, by teaching Web evaluation, at least they may consider and question authority of sites.

In several 15 to 20-minute sessions, demonstrate various points in your Web evaluation guide of choice or use the following Web Evaluation Guide developed by Kathy Schrock <http://school.discovery.com/schrockguide/evalmidd.html>, especially focusing on accuracy of content and authority of the author, using examples and non-examples from the Web. In a lab setting, put students in groups of two or three, providing a Web site to identify the studied components. Instead of teaching all points in one long session, breaking the Web Evaluation Guide into short sections will keep students' attention and interest. In order for the teacher or library media specialist to ensure that students are deliberately thinking about sites they use, the student must evaluate the site before it is used in the assignment and turn in the evaluation.

Use a Wiki to Support Information Seeking Strategies

See Chapter Six for introduction to using wikis.

Project wiki: A list of sources appears on the Information Seeking Strategy page for the project wiki (Figure 7.4). You can link Web sites you want students to use, as well as include book titles, subscription databases, and other sources of information. The list of sources can be added after the class brainstorms and selects its titles (see the introductory activity above). If the teacher wishes to save time, he can post the list and explain to the class why he chose those particular titles.

Group wikis: Student groups can use their Information Seeking Strategies wiki page to brainstorm their initial list of sources, revising the list with your guidance. This is especially beneficial if groups will use sources different from other groups. If all groups will use basically the same sources, they can copy and paste the list from the project page to their own.

Figure 7.4: Project Wiki: Information Seeking Strategies

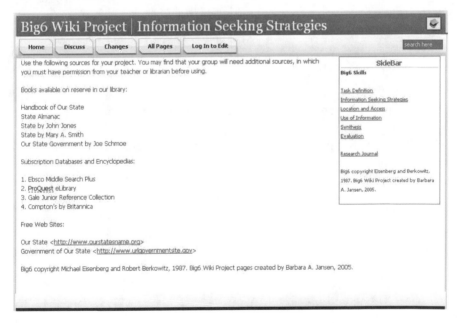

Specific Uses of Technology for Information Seeking Strategies

Figure 7.5: Possible Uses of Technology for Information Seeking Strategies

Information Seeking Strategies	Possible technologies used
#2.1 Brainstorm possible sources	Class project: Use a wiki to list sources needed. Groups of students use their wikis to brainstorm sources needed for their project. They copy and paste additional sources from the project wiki. Students can use word processing to brainstorm a list of possible sources. Students browse subscription databases to add to list; show them to find out the contents of each database.
#2.2 Select best sources	Show students pre-selected free Web sites that they will use and explain the criteria used for the selection. Show selected subscription databases and explain why they are the best to use for this topic.

Works Cited

Lauer, Diane. "Re: permission requested." E-mail to Barbara Jansen. 28 February 06.

Schrock, Kathy. Re: permission requested." E-mail to Barbara Jansen. 28 March 06.

Chapter 8

Location and Access

L ocating sources and the information contained within sources
continues to challenge middle school students. They are used to getting
immediate results by changing the channel or speeding through
commercials on a TV program saved to their digital video recorder.
Convincing students that they must practice patience may be our greatest
challenge. Once we guide students in identifying best sources, educators
may erroneously assume middle school students have the skills necessary to
locate those sources. There are several reasons many students cannot
achieve this step without extensive assistance:

- Whether the student is locating a book or Web site, a 10-15 year-old
child's level of cognitive development may be too immature for the multi-
step process required to find a resource, especially one on the free or fee-
based Web.

- A student must be able to spell correctly if independently using the
library's online catalog or if searching within a subject directory,
database, or search engine.

- The vast number of books on library shelves, of returns from a search of the
online catalog, and of results from a search of a subscription database can
overwhelm a student to the point of rendering her helpless and ineffective.

Additionally, a student typically learns how to read with fiction, therefore
having little experience with nonfiction and in knowing how to read for
information, including using tables of content and indices to locate specific
information within a source. Focused planning and frequent teaching of various

location skills, as well as providing students with numerous opportunities to practice locating materials and accessing the information within will ease, but not eliminate, the difficult nature of this step.

Get Started

Introduce Location and Access to Students: Plan

Big6 #3.1: Locate Sources

Begin planning for instruction by reviewing the sources of information identified in Information Seeking Strategies. Group sources by format such as books, encyclopedias, Web sites, and formats contained in subscription services or databases (most contain multiple information formats—overview articles, newspaper and magazine articles, images, primary sources, reference, among others). Consider spending only 15-20 minutes instructing students in any location skill, because more time for instruction does not necessarily equal greater understanding. Repeat or review lessons as needed in subsequent days or units.

Books and encyclopedias: Decide if you will put books on reserve or if students will locate the books they need. For group projects, putting books on reserve will ensure that each class has access to the books at point of need. For individual projects, especially those in which students choose their own topics, having students locate needed books may be the most effective course of action. Determine if students have the skills to use the online public access or card catalog (see additional strategies in this chapter for an activity on the library's catalog). You may want to review or demonstrate the use of keyword or subject searching and library shelf arrangement. Understanding Boolean searching (using *and*, *or*, *not*) will help students broaden or narrow their searches (see activity in this chapter). Middle school students should have had instruction in elementary school on the arrangement of the library, but don't assume that they are proficient at these skills. An overview of the Dewey Decimal System and its arrangement in your library may be needed for students to navigate the collection successfully.

Online subscription services and databases, including online encyclopedias: Planning for student access to subscription databases requires you to make several determinations.

■ How will students locate the service, database, or encyclopedia—links on your library's or district's Web pages, bookmarks on each computer's Internet browsers, or icons on the computer's desktop? Do students need passwords at school or at home?

■ If accessing databases through a service such as Thomson Gale™, EBSCOHost®, SIRS®, or ProQuest® (which include multiple databases), determine which databases within the service students will use to access needed information.

Free Web sites: How will students locate sites on the free Web? You can link to sites through your class or library's Web pages, bookmark your classroom and library computers with the sites that you want students to use, or use a uniform resource locator (URL) organizer service such as TrackStar <http://trackstar.4teachers.org/trackstar>. If you want students to locate sites, your library may have a subscription to a subject directory such as netTrekker or WebFeet <http://www.webfeetguides.com>.

The editors (often teachers and library media specialists) of these subscription directories evaluate free Web sites for accuracy and authority and categorize them into appropriate subject headings and grade levels, and, as with netTrekker, add value by correlating the Web sites to state curriculum standards and reading levels; include timelines, person, and image searches; add sites that support English language learners, and much more. Free subject directories, such as KidsClick <http://www.kidsclick.org> or Great Web Sites for Kids <http://www.ala.org/greatsites/>, also allow students to access sites evaluated and categorized by library media specialists or editors. Decide how you will direct students to the Web directory and determine the path needed to access the appropriate Web sites within. Students can also browse these directories.

Other sources such as subject-area experts, audio and video, or personal observation: Determine which introductory level skills students need to locate the source and plan how you will teach the skill to the students.

Big6 #3.2: Accessing Information within Sources

Books: By fifth or sixth grade, students should know how to use the table of contents and index. Record the steps that you will guide the class through to review these skills and make the appropriate visual displays for instruction.

Encyclopedias on the shelf: Selecting an encyclopedia volume by topic should not challenge most middle school students. Learning to use the index may require direct teaching. Rather than teach students to use each encyclopedia index, teach the concept of indexing, as the index may vary slightly among titles. Teaching the concept will transfer to other indexes that students will encounter, such as textbooks, almanacs, and A-Z indexes that are becoming increasingly common in subscription databases and free Web sites. Explain to students that indexes may look different, but they all have the same arrangement (a detailed list arranged alphabetically) and function (to help a reader find information quickly). Instead of inefficiently flipping through the pages of a book, the index indicates an exact page number. See additional strategies for a simple activity to illustrate indexing.

Online subscription databases and encyclopedias: Once students locate the appropriate database, what do they need to know to begin using it to locate articles and other information formats? For introductory purposes, consider using the simple or basic search feature (as opposed to the advanced search).

Experiment with various combinations of keywords and related words students identified in Task Definition in the simple search to determine which combination returns the best results. Make note of those keyword combinations and relevant article titles to tell students, as it is easy to forget when you actually instruct. See the Additional Strategies section for lesson ideas in database searching.

Deliver Instruction
Big6 #3.1 and #3.2

Display the Big6 chart and direct students' attention to Big6 #3: Location and Access, specifically #3.1: Locate Sources. Review the list of sources determined in Big6 #2.2. Discuss the location of each. Demonstrate the location of sources and have students practice as needed and appropriate. Repeat the sequence for Big6 #3.2: Access Information within the Source.

Additional Strategies for Engaging Students in Location and Access

Teach the Concept of Indexing

Have students compare the index in their textbook with one in an encyclopedia. Answer the following questions: How are the indexes alike? Different? What information can you get from an index? When should you use an index? How is an index different from a table of contents? Now have students compare and contrast the indexes of two different encyclopedia titles. Most middle school students will easily grasp the concept of indexing after interacting with several examples.

Use Boolean Operators

Try this simple activity to help students understand the concept of Boolean operators:

Baking Pizzas

Preparation:

Cut white drawing paper into large circles—one circle for each group. Prepare cards containing this text (make enough cards for the combinations below, or create your own).

AND	pepperoni	black olives	green peppers
OR	mushrooms	onions	Italian sausage
NOT	green olives	Canadian bacon	ground beef

Activity:

1. Separate class into groups of 2, 3, or 4.

2. Give each group a circle and markers or crayons.

3. Tell the class that they are baking pizzas to sell. Each group should think of a name for its restaurant (optional). Give each group one of the following orders by placing the appropriate cards on its table (tell students that all the pizzas have cheese and tomato sauce):

- Group One: pepperoni AND mushrooms AND black olives

- Group Two: Italian sausage OR pepperoni AND green peppers

- Group Three: Canadian bacon AND onions AND green olives

- Group Four: ground beef OR Italian sausage AND mushrooms NOT onions

- Group Five: mushrooms AND green olives AND onions NOT ground beef

- Group Six: black olives OR green olives AND Canadian bacon

4. Give students enough time to draw and color their pizzas.

5. Have each group explain and show what it put on its pizza. Discuss how the operators AND, OR, NOT help to broaden or narrow the results.

6. If time permits, collect the Boolean cards in one stack and the pizza ingredients in another stack, turning the stacks upside down. Have each group select two Boolean cards and three ingredient cards. If they get two of the same ingredient, tell them that they will just put double the ingredient! Groups create another pizza according to the combination of cards they drew.

7. Tell students that searching by keywords in the online card catalog or in databases and search engines is like making pizza, except instead of using dough and ingredients, they will be searching for books, documents, or Web sites that contain a combination of subjects.

Review the concept of Boolean operators by holding up the cards and asking students to give examples, such as books that contain information about dogs OR cats (more); books that contain information about dogs AND cats (more); books that contain information about dogs NOT pit bulls (fewer).

Search the School Library's Catalog

Middle school students in grades six through eight who matriculated from a strong library program in elementary school will know how to navigate the library's online public access catalog (OPAC). However, not all elementary programs provide a strong foundation in using the OPAC or in accessing materials on the shelf. The library media specialist may need to teach classes of students the nuances of using the catalog to locate materials housed in the library's physical collection for academic and personal needs. Teach students when to choose among various search options:

Author: Use when searching for materials by a known author.

Title: Use when searching for a known title.

Subject: Use when a general topic is sought, e.g., civil rights or solar system.

Keyword: Use when combining topics. Boolean searching may be implemented.

Series: Use when searching for a known series, such as R. L. Stine's *Fear Street.*

Other options may be added depending on the library's automation software.

Effective lessons are taught in 15 to 20 minutes at point of need in the curriculum. Middle school students should catch on quickly and be able to transfer the concepts to their public library's OPAC as well.

Search within a Subscription Database

Basic search or advanced search? Full-text, subject, keyword, subject index, author, source, or document type? Searching subscription databases is difficult and tedious for even adults. Intuition fails us, as the search terms seem confusing and complicated. Understanding basic and advanced searching will help return effective results. Typical fifth and sixth graders will use the *simple or basic search* (the default search screen), as will most seventh through ninth graders. Simple or basic search usually defaults to a subject search, but may also allow for keyword or full-text choices. (See Figure 8.1 for an explanation of terms.) Also, many databases allow for browsing by subject, which may prove effective for young searchers, because database searching requires correct spelling and complex terminology for best results. Consider introducing the *advanced search* in seventh or eighth grade, giving students ample opportunities to practice. Most will not master the skill of advanced searching, but can gain an understanding of its various concepts. Be aware, however, that the components of most advanced searches will be confusing to even some ninth graders and may result in confusion and frustration. Introducing advanced search strategies a few at a time may result in less frustration. Figure 8.1 defines various search terms.

Advanced Search Terms used in middle school databases by Gale, ProQuest, SIRS, and EBSCO (these vary by database, not all included in each)	
Term	**Meaning**
Subject, subject terms, subject headings, subject list	Created by indexers or editors, subjects are assigned, based on controlled vocabulary, often associated with Library of Congress subject headings. Most useful for single topic searches and returns the most on-target results (Cardwell, 2006).
Keyword	Keyword searching allows for the user to combine several topics or subjects in one search. Looks for the terms in certain parts of the article, such as the title, citation, abstract, subject headings, and as in Gale databases, searches the first 50 words in the article. Returns a larger set of results than subject searching (Cardwell, 2006).
Natural language	Allows the searcher to enter a question or full phrase. The database will ignore unimportant words such as *the, of, for, after*. ProQuest's eLibrary allows for natural language searching.
Full-text, all text, text word (all words except stopwords)	Searches all text of the document for the terms. If a choice is made to search for articles with full-text this means that the database also contains citations or abstracts; full-text searching in this case returns only complete articles or documents.
Boolean	Allows use of AND, OR, NOT to limit searches.
Title, headline	Searches title or headline for terms.
Author	Searches for works by a particular author. If students are looking for information about an author, they should search by subject.
Geographical Terms	Searches for place.
Abstract	Searches the abstract of an article.
ISSN, ISBN	Searches for the International Standard Serial Number or the International Standards Book Number.
Journal name, journal search	Searches for a particular journal title.
Date	Allows searcher to search for articles published within certain dates or by a single date.
Source	Searches for a particular source such as a magazine or reference work.
Content Index	Allows the searcher to locate all records with images, full text, or abstracts, eliminating those without.
Record number	A letter-number combination that uniquely identifies each record.

> **TIP** **Print Articles from Databases**
>
> All subscription databases have a feature that allows for clean printing. If you allow students to print from databases, show students how an article looks before and after choosing the print feature. It strips unnecessary graphics and headings, saving paper and toner. Students will find highlighting and note taking more effective when reading from a clean article that has more white space for marking and taking notes.

Use Advanced Search Strategies for Google™ and Other Search Engines

Students love to search the Web and feel confident using various search engines. However, observation shows us that students, content to use the default simple search, return results in the hundreds of thousands—even well over one million—making searching time consuming, tedious, and difficult to find a relevant link. For better results, show students in grades seven through nine how to use the advanced search (including grades five and six, if allowing them to search for their own sites).

In a lab setting, have students access the Google Web site <http://www.google.com>. Take them through the following steps:

1. Type george washington in the simple search field. (How many hits are returned?)
2. Click on Advanced search. Delete george washington.
3. In the field **With exact phrase** type: george washington. (How many hits?) Notice quotation marks in search bar. Go back to Advanced search.
4. In the field **Without the words** type: university. (How many hits?) Notice the minus sign in the search bar. Go back to Advanced search.
5. In the field **With all of the words** type: president. (How many hits?)

Students should easily see that by using the advanced search, they can obtain more focused results, even though they will still retrieve an over-whelming number of results.

Use a Wiki to Support Location and Access

See Chapter Six for introduction to using wikis.

Project wiki: The teacher will include any specific directions and strategies for locating and accessing specific sources. She may also want each group to record keywords on the Location and Access pages of their group wikis (Figure 8.2).

Group wikis: Each group member creates a Location and Access page on which to record keywords and related words for essential points of access, such as titles, captions, and topic sentences (see Chapter Nine for an explanation of essential points of access). Each student can make notes on strategies he will use for locating sources or use the page to keep track of sources he is currently using in order to return to them in later research sessions. He may also wish to make notes on sources he is having trouble locating or difficulty accessing the information needed.

Figure 8.2: Project Wiki: Location and Access

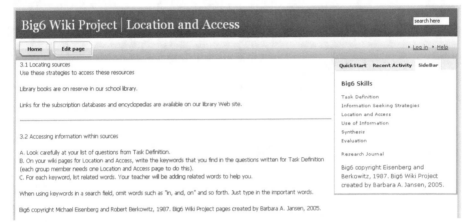

Specific Uses of Technology to Support Location and Access

Figure 8.3: Possible Uses of Technology in Location and Access

Information Seeking Strategies	Possible technologies used
3.1 Brainstorm possible sources	Use the class project wiki to provide strategies and links to accessing sources. Students can use their group wiki page to divide and assign members to search various book and electronic sources. Individuals and groups can search subject directories—free and subscription, subscription databases, and the school's online catalog to search for sources of needed information. Under supervision students use a search engine for sites on the free Web.
3.2 Access information within source	Finding articles within a subscription database: Students try various combinations of their keyword and related words in the simple search of the database. Motivated students can use the features of the database's advanced search capabilities such as subject, keyword, and full-text searching. Once relevant articles are located, students use the Edit … Find feature in their computer's Internet browser to locate essential points of access. (There is some cross-over from Big6 #3.2 to #4.1.)

Work Cited:

Cardwell, Vanessa. "RE: question about terminology." E-mail to Barbara Jansen. 24 Feb 2006.

The

BIG

6

Chapter 9

Use of Information

One student has the encyclopedia open to the correct page, another's Web page displays the answers needed for questions written in the Task Definition stage of the process. However, neither can identify the relevant information. What is the missing link between the student's information need and recognizing that the words on the page satisfy the need? Most likely, she cannot make the connection between the words on the page and the words she and her teacher used to form the questions to be answered. To a student's question, "When was Coretta Scott King born?," a reference source may just give the dates when someone was born instead of stating "Coretta Scott King was born on Feb. 21, 1921." An encyclopedia will cover a state's economic resources, not as an easily recognizable list: Economic resources are cattle, cotton and oil, and farming, but in narrative form such as, "Cattle and cotton dominated the economy of Texas before oil was discovered. Texas remains one of the nation's most productive farming states. It often leads all other states in the production of cotton and the raising of beef cattle. Corn, sorghum, wheat, rice, and oats are also important crops. In addition to cattle, the state's livestock includes sheep, chickens, turkeys, pigs, and horses" (Texas, 2006). The teacher must help students make the connection by helping them identify keywords and related words "What do we mean by 'economic resources?' Look for things like domesticated animals, technology, logging, farming, agriculture, water, minerals, oil, and manufacturing." The students should write the list in a contrasting color below the corresponding question on their note taking organizer so those terms are available at point of need. Keywords and related words may be generated in Task Definition (see Chapter Six) and further expanded in Use of Information as needed.

Get Started

Introduce Use of Information to Students: Plan

Big6 #4.1: Engage in the Source

For students to find information within sources, they need to begin by identifying keywords and related words (see Identify Keywords in Chapter Six). Engaging in the source begins with learning how to "read" a page of information, whether it is from a bound book or encyclopedia or from a page of electronic text and graphics. Students must identify those *essential points of access* such as title and subtitles, topic sentences in each paragraph, labels and captions, bold and italicized words of importance, graphics, icons, tabs, and links. Students should also learn to recognize and ignore advertising and other non-essential clutter on a page.

In planning for instruction, consider the ability a student needs to scan a page for the essential points of access and in looking for keywords and related words. Plan to demonstrate scanning for the essential points of access by using a projection of an encyclopedia page or a page from an electronic subscription database. If you do not have a projection device available for a computer, print the page and make an overhead transparency. You may need to enlarge these copies so all students can see the text and give students a photocopy of the article or page to follow. Try to demonstrate on a related topic instead of an exact topic that students will research. For example, if students are studying the state's notable historical persons, use a related person from another state or era. Write a list of information needed in question form (from Task Definition in Chapter Six), including a set of keywords and related words for your example.

Big6 #4.2: Extract Relevant Information

In preparation for your demonstration, decide what type of notes students will take (knowledge level, summary, or paraphrase—see Additional Strategies in this chapter for ideas about note taking instruction). Make a visual that you will display of the note taking organizer the students will use. Determine the instruction students will need in citing sources.

Deliver Instruction

Big6 #4.1: Engage in the Source

The following steps will help students understand how to identify essential points of access and to locate and extract needed information.

1. Display the Big6 chart and direct students' attention to Big6 #4: Use of Information, specifically #4.1: Engage in the Source.

2. Display your list of information needed and the set of accompanying keywords and related words. Tell students that once they have located the information within the source, it is time to identify essential points of access for the information needed, using the keywords and related words they generated in Task Definition. Choose a question for which you will look for the "answer."

3. Display the page of information from a book, encyclopedia, or subscription database that you prepared.

4. **Skimming**
   Show students how you skim for *essential points of access* by identifying titles and subtitles, reading topic sentences of paragraphs, looking at sections, labels, captions, graphics and icons, tabs, and links—whatever is appropriate for that page. Do this for both pages (encyclopedia and electronic). Skimming requires the reader to read quickly and look for main ideas or supporting details in a paragraph (Phipps 4-5). Skimming requires the reader to take in large chunks of text at one time. The reader is concerned with getting an idea of the whole passage. Comprehension does not depend on reading every word. Teach students to read the first and last paragraphs of sections for summaries of the content, and the first and last sentences of paragraphs to gain an impression of the topic (Cheek and Collins).

5. Have the students follow along with their fingers on the copies you provided. If you do not have to use the copies for another class, have students circle the essential points of access as you demonstrate.

6. Once you finish circling all essential points of access, identify one that points to a section that will answer one of your questions. Show students how it either contains words directly from the question or has a keyword or related word.

7. Tell students that once an appropriate section is located, one that hopefully answers a question, then they will read in more detail for the information they need to take out (Big6 #4.2).

8. **Scanning**
   Inform students that the skill used to locate answers to specific questions is called scanning and actually requires that they read more of the text than they did when skimming for essential points of access. Scanning requires the student to "move his or her eyes quickly over a piece of reading material looking for one specific point, the words they are looking for jump off the page at them. It is employed for pinpointing needed facts or ideas from the text or the index. It involves skipping words, but the emphasis is on recognition. The reader knows what to look for and rapidly scans until words are found and closer reading can occur" (Phipps 4-5). Show students how you read most of the words in the paragraph, looking for those words that answer a question.

9. **Big6 #4.2: Extract Relevant Information—Note Taking**
   It is here that you will instruct the class in the "trash and treasure" note taking strategy if students do not know how to record knowledge-level or factual information (see Additional Strategies in this chapter).

10. Underline or highlight words that answer a question, then record just the needed words and phrases on the note taking organizer. Have students follow your lead with the highlighting of the needed information on their copy of the page.

11. If the amount of information needed is greater than several words or phrases, demonstrate summarizing or paraphrasing on the note taking organizer (see Additional Strategies in this chapter).

12. In groups, have students use their copy to search for the "answer" to another question. Check and discuss. Practice several times as needed.

Citing Sources

Demonstrate how to cite the source on the note taking organizer. Consider citing the source as soon as the demonstration page is displayed so students form good note taking and citing habits. Using a free (as of this printing) online service such at Citation Machine <http://citationmachine.net> or EasyBib <http://www.easybib.com> takes the tedium out of citing sources. Certainly, middle school students will continue to struggle with citing subscription databases, free Web sites, and other sources due to the difficulty of locating the statements of responsibility and other pertinent information. Be prepared to help students fill in the blanks.

Additional Strategies for Engaging Students in Use of Information

Note Taking

Once the section containing needed information is recognized, middle school researchers usually copy the entire paragraph word for word, when they only need a phrase or two. Library media specialists and teachers often tell students not to copy "word for word," but to "put it in your own words." We should understand that children this age may not completely comprehend specific words and phrases, and their limited vocabularies restrict the ability to effectively paraphrase. Many times, the kind of information children this age typically need is facts or dates—common knowledge, not information that needs to be paraphrased (or even cited for that matter). According to Stripling and Pitts, there are four types of notes a student can take: citation (facts, statistics, dates, etc.), summary, paraphrase, and quotation. Fifth and sixth grade students will use citation and possibly summary when taking notes from sources. While many of our state standards require that students summarize and paraphrase and our state exams require that students recognize summary and paraphrase, this is developmentally difficult for students 10-13 (and often 14-15) years of age to actually compose on their own. The following strategies should help introduce to students the various types of note taking.

Trash and Treasure Note Taking Method

Using the "trash and treasure" method to instruct researchers in middle grades on citation level (or knowledge level) note taking not only helps students identify the needed sections of a reference source, but also specific words to extract for their stated purpose.

Direct instruction is necessary the first few times students are required to take notes for an assignment. Frequent review helps students become independent users of the process. Relate note taking to a pirate's treasure map (show one if necessary—a Google™ search will return a number of treasure maps, or draw a rough one). The map itself is like the article or chapter of a book containing information about the topic. The X on the map, which marks the exact location of the buried treasure, is the section of the text containing needed information or "answers" for specific questions defined in Task Definition. A pirate or treasure hunter must dig for the chest, shoveling aside "trash"—dirt, weeds, and rocks. A researcher must dig to find the "treasure"—words that help answer the questions. He or she must "shovel aside" unnecessary sentences, phrases, and words (trash words). Of course, these words are not trash to the original source, only to the researcher, because they do not answer the questions defined in the task. Demonstrate this concept using a projected image of an encyclopedia article or section. The students should each have a copy of the article so they can follow along and practice the technique.

1. Show a prepared question, including the underlined keywords and list of related words.
2. Skim the article for *essential points of access* until you locate the appropriate heading or section.
3. Place a slash at the end of the first sentence and read it. Ask "Does this sentence answer the question?"
4. If the answer is no, tell the students that this sentence is "trash" to them. Go on to the next sentence, placing a slash at the end.
5. If the answer is yes, underline the first phrase and ask if that phrase answers the question. If the answer is no, underline the next phrase and repeat the question.
6. If the answer is yes, read that phrase word-by-word, asking which words are needed to answer the question—treasure words. Circle those words, then write them in the appropriate place on the projected data chart or whichever organizer the students are using. Those that do not answer the question are trash words. Continue phrase by phrase and word by word

until the end of the sentence. Count the words in the sentence and then count the treasure words. Students are very impressed when you say, "The sentence has 17 words and I only needed to write four of them. I don't know about you, but I would rather write four than 17!"

7. Demonstrate the process again, allowing the students to practice, using copies of the article. Allow students to independently practice a few times before they begin their own research. The library media specialist and teacher should monitor each student's work, reteaching as necessary.

Once students understand the concept of "trash and treasure" words, they begin to write fewer and fewer unnecessary words.

Summarize Information

When reading a large section for overall meaning, students should use summarizing to condense the main ideas into one to three sentences. Summarizing is typically used for beginning research, i.e., general explanatory material (Stripling and Pitts, 1988). Use these steps to teach middle school children how to summarize:

1. Locate a relevant section with several paragraphs.

2. Read first relevant paragraph. Write the main idea and list the most important supporting details.

3. Repeat for all paragraphs.

4. Now look at the main idea of each paragraph. What is the overall main idea of this section?

5. Summarize the section by writing a short paragraph that includes the overall main idea and the main ideas of each paragraph.

Paraphrase Information

Due to students changing ideas into "their own words," paraphrasing is the note taking form most likely to result in plagiarism, as many students do not know that they must use quotations around those words they used directly from the source, as well as cite it, even if they changed all words. In addition, paraphrasing remains beyond what a typical fifth or sixth grader (and many seventh, eighth, and ninth graders) can accomplish. We should understand that children this age may not completely comprehend specific words and phrases, and their growing vocabularies may restrict the ability to paraphrase effectively. Use paraphrasing for supporting information, biographical information, predictions, hypothesis, and drawing conclusions. Unlike summarizing, paraphrased notes do not leave out any information.
Use the following steps to instruct academically ready students in the skill of paraphrasing.

1. Read the original text as many times as needed to understand its full meaning.
2. Pretend that you have to explain it to a younger person who won't understand the original. What would you say?
3. Write your explanation in your own words (paraphrase) on your note taking organizer.
4. Make sure that you have included most of the information that you read in the original text. Almost all of the information in the original text will be included in your paraphrase, but in your words. This is not the same as a summary that will have only the important points.
5. Use quotation marks to identify any words you have borrowed directly from the source.
6. Record the source (including the page) on your note taking organizer so that you can find it easily if you choose to use the ideas in your paper or project.

Reinforce Summarizing and Paraphrasing

Practice, practice, practice! Efficient note taking requires repeated efforts. The following activity will provide a structured practice session for summarizing and paraphrasing. Choose two short newspaper articles from the newspaper dated the day of or day before the lesson. They should interest the students and contain three to five paragraphs. Make enough copies of the first article for each group, and the second article for each student. Separate the class into groups of three or four. Discuss or review summarizing and the steps involved. Have each group summarize the article. Each group should read its summary, having the class critique it according to the steps of effective summaries (listed above). Follow the same directions for paraphrasing, using the same article. Discuss each group's effort and compare to the steps of an effective paraphrase (listed above). Hand out the second article and have students summarize and paraphrase it on their own. Discuss their results. Consider having students turn in their work so that you can individually assess and help those still in need. One or two days later, review and reteach for those students who do not understand the concepts of summarizing and paraphrasing.

Compare Information from More Than One Source

State standardized test items may require that students compare information found from various sources (Figure 9.1). Give students meaningful practice by having them use the following chart to record notes.

Figure 9.1: Comparing Information from More Than One Source

Question	Notes	Similarities	Differences
Source 1			
Source 2			
Source 3			

Consider Electronic Note Taking

Taking notes electronically using a word processor is a natural extension of students' familiarity with the computer. Keyboarding classes and sending text and instant messages make many of today's students very fast typists. Of course, students who do not have cell phones and Internet access at home may be at a disadvantage, but electronic note taking in middle school provides meaningful practice on the keyboard they might not have otherwise.

Numerous benefits make electronic note taking appealing. Students can copy and paste words or short phrases from sources into an electronic graphic organizer. Printer usage may be lessened if students can copy and paste needed words and phrases instead of highlighting words on printed Web pages and databases. Students can electronically save Web pages for further use, easily deleting them when finished. They can integrate summarized and paraphrased notes into the final paper or project. By eighth or ninth grade, students may need to reorganize or categorize notes, and can do so with less tedium. Middle schoolers often have difficulty keeping track of papers; if their notes are stored electronically, especially on a file server, the notes are safe and accessible from any computer on campus. In addition to note taking, the computer simplifies the process of citing sources and creating a bibliography.

Hand-written notes have their own benefits. Some teachers may feel that students will think about what they write if required to write by hand and will be less likely to write huge amounts of unneeded text. The act of forming the letters and words may help students remember what they have written. All children have access to pencil and paper at school, but all children in a class may not have access to a computer. The careful educator will weigh the benefits of handwritten and electronic note taking to make the right decision for students in his classroom.

Use Note Taking Organizers

Students may use the following note taking organizers electronically using a word processor or with hand-written notes. They are easily created on the computer or simply by folding, printing, or drawing.

Data Chart

A data chart (Figure 9.2) is useful for recording factual and knowledge-level notes. It keeps all notes from all sources together on one page, which may be considered a drawback if children need to reorganize or categorize notes in Big6 #5.1: Organizing Information from Multiple Sources. Each student folds a piece of large white drawing paper into 16 boxes. The creases form the borders of the boxes. Inserting a table in a word processor (choosing landscape view), with four columns and four rows, accomplishes the same thing. Students record notes for knowledge-level information in the appropriate boxes. There is enough space for them to answer seven questions (three on front and four on back). If they have more to answer, you may want to re-think the number of questions or use a different note taking organizer.

Figure 9.2: Data Chart

Student's name Topic Date	Question 1	Question 2	Question 3
Source 1	Notes from source 1 for question 1	Notes from source 1 for question 2	Notes from source 1 for question 3
Source 2	Notes from source 2 for question 1	Notes from source 2 for question 2	Notes from source 2 for question 3
Source 3 or summary			

Figure 9.3: Graphic Organizer for Recording Main Idea and Supporting Details

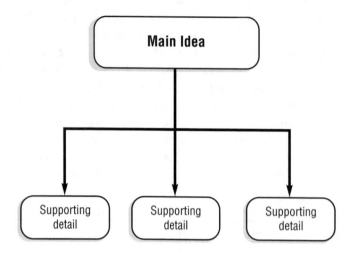

Example for ninth grade group studying Islam:

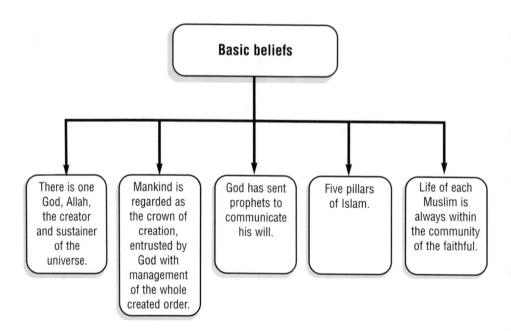

Note Taking Form Created with Word Processor

The form below (Figure 9.4) can be added as a template to any computer using Microsoft Word or other word processing program. Create the form using a table, then add it to the templates for new documents. Typically, you save the table as a template which will add it to the template's folder, making it accessible when creating a new document.

Figure 9.4 Note Taking Form

Student's name	
Today's date	
Source (title, author, publication, date, URL)	
Subject	
Notes (Important information—copy and paste words or short, factual phrases; summarize; paraphrase; avoid copying and pasting huge blocks of text.) Put quotes "" around words or phrases that are copied directly from the source. Include ways you may use the material or help you need.	

Use PowerPoint for Recording Notes

While PowerPoint is often overused or used ineffectively as a way for students to present the results of information searching, it can act as a powerful note taking organizer (Figure 9.5). Students can easily add new slides when their source or topic changes. They can store notes and images, and create citation slides. Slides can be organized and re-ordered, printed, or made into outlines. Students can color-code the slides or the text of notes that belong to a particular source. PowerPoint can act as note cards, as students can cut the slides apart with scissors.

Figure 9.5: Using PowerPoint for Note Taking

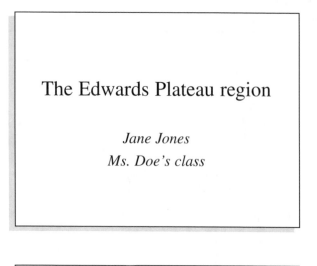

What is the land like?

- many springs, stony hills, and steep canyons
- grasslands and savannah
- landscape is rolling to hilly and elevation ranges from 825 to 2,250 feet above sea level
- Texas Parks and Wildlife Web site

What are the industries?

- Ranching
- Manufacturing
- High tech—semiconductors

What is the climate?

- Average annual rainfall ranges from 15 to 34 inches
- Moderate temperatures in winter
- Hot and humid in summer
- Mild fall and spring

What animals live here?

What plants grow here?

What is important
about this area?

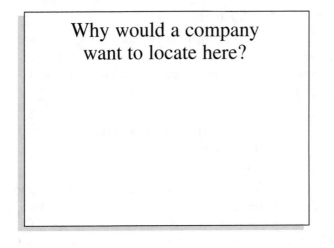

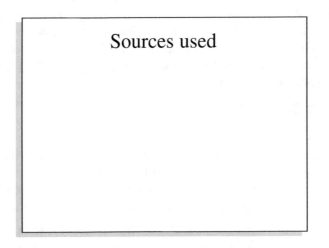

Note Taking from Other Sources

Interviews: Students should prepare questions for the interviewee during the Task Definition step of the process. Making an audio or video recording of the interview allows for a smoother session and provides an accurate record for students to transcribe at their own pace after the interview.

Video: Teachers should stop the video at appropriate points and ask the students what was important, requiring them to record notes at that time. Middle school students probably do not have the skills or speed needed to take notes as the video continues to play.

Lecture or oral presentations: The presenter should emphasize important points and allow students time to record those points or write the important notes on the board for students to record after the presentation. Providing an outline with space for recording notes will aid students and keep them on task. Middle school students may not have the necessary skills to take notes during a presentation—they often miss several minutes of the lecture as they try to record notes. You may want to ask the guest speaker to provide an outline or pause after important points to allow students to take notes. Some speakers may also allow themselves to be recorded for later playback. However, you will need to obtain the speaker's permission.

Use a Wiki to Support Use of Information

See Chapter Six for introduction to using wikis.

Project wiki: After demonstrating or reviewing appropriate note taking methods, record the kind of notes that students should take (knowledge-level, summary, or paraphrase) as in Figure 9.6. Upload the note taking form that students will use, if not taking notes on their group wiki.

Group wikis: Students can use their group wikis to record notes, or use the note taking form provided by the teacher. If they use the wiki to record notes, each student needs separate pages. Their Use of Information wiki pages also allow for determining ways in which they will use the notes they took from sources, or to keep track of sources used. Students within a group can communicate to others about which sources hold information for various group members. Students can also communicate with their teacher if help is needed. The wiki can serve as a bookmark so that students will know where they should start taking notes in the next research session.

Figure 9.6 Project Wiki: Use of Information

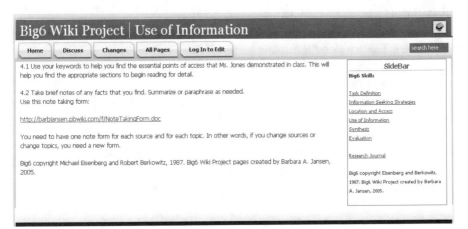

Specific Uses of Technology for Use of Information

Figure 9.7: Possible Uses for Technology in Use of Information

Use of information	Possible technologies used
4.1 Engage in the source	Class wiki project page: Give students directions or review on using their keywords and related words to find essential points of access. Upload to the wiki page the note taking form you want students to use or allow them to use the group wiki to record their notes. Use the Edit-Find feature in the computer's Internet browser to find keywords and related words on the page.
4.2 Extract needed information	Students use their group wiki pages to record notes. Each student can create his or her own wiki pages on the group wiki to record notes. Groups and individual students use word processing, Inspiration™ Software, or PowerPoint to record notes. Copy and paste words and short factual phrases to note taking organizer. Use electronic citation services to cite sources, such as <http://citationmachine.net>.

Works Cited:

Cheek, Earl H., Jr. and Martha D. Collins. *Strategies for Reading.* Columbus: Charles E. Merrill Publishing Company, 1985.

Phipps, Rita. *The Successful Student's Handbook: A Step-By-Step Guide to Study, Reading, and Thinking Skills.* Seattle and London: University of Washington Press, 1983.

Stripling, Barbara K. and Judy M. Pitts. *Brainstorms and Blueprints: Teaching Library Research as a Thinking Process.* Englewood, Colorado: Libraries Unlimited, Inc., 1988.

"Texas." *Britannica Elementary Encyclopedia.* 2006. *Encyclopædia Britannica Online School Edition.* 10 Apr 2006 <http://school.eb.com/elementary/article?articleId=345528>.

Chapter 10

Synthesis

Too often, results of the research process end in superficial products, such as the seventh grade class that makes sugar cube igloos after studying the Inuits, or sixth graders constructing mobiles made of coat hangers, dangling facts about endangered animals, or ninth graders studying ancient Egypt create PowerPoint presentations containing facts and pictures copied from Internet sites. Projects similar to these abound in grades five through nine. Teachers and library media specialists instruct students in finding information, even using the Big6, but accept final products and papers that add no value through higher-level thinking or original ideas.

Figure 10.1: A Cautionary Statement

> ## ! Barbara Jansen's Cautionary Statement
>
> Assigning children traditional copy-and-paste research reports will extinguish their natural enthusiam for discovery and will encourage "copying from the encylopedia."
>
> Does this mean that teachers should not assign reports? No! It just means that the final product should provide students with the ability to add value to their educational experience by contributing original ideas and higher-level thought, in addition to learning transferable skills.
>
> In other words...
>
> What can students do when they are finished with the final product that they could not do when they started it?

Go Beyond the Facts

Getting students to process the facts and other information they find using higher-level thought and original ideas will result in a final product that represents the best of what that student can offer. It will stretch a student's intellect and engage her in the learning process. When she adds personal value to the results, she takes more ownership and pride in her work. Going beyond the facts means that a student will have to use higher-level skills to process the information found in sources, instead of just rewriting or copying and pasting those facts into a report or other product.

How would this final project look to a sixth grader? After finding facts about an endangered animal, the student writes a letter to the city council or to the editor of the local paper telling about this animal and why its habitat should be preserved. In addition to answering questions such as, What does this animal eat? What predators does this animal have? In which type of habitat does this animal live?, students are also answering, How is this animal important to the environment? How does it contribute to its habitat? How might the habitat change if the animal were no longer living there? Why do you think this animal's habitat should be preserved? How do you feel about construction ruining this animal's habitat? Sixth graders could even begin practicing presentation skills by presenting their findings and ideas in a mock city council meeting.

How does "going beyond the facts" look to a ninth grader? Finding facts and graphics on ancient Egypt on the Internet and in library books takes students through Use of Information. Instead of having students copy and paste to PowerPoint slides, have students in groups by topic (daily life in Ancient Egypt; burial customs; religion, beliefs, and roles of deities; and government) pretend to be consultants to "Universe Pictures," an imaginary movie studio producing The Mummy III: The Pharoah's Dynasty. They must present, to the producer, their ideas on how to make the movie historically accurate, and give suggestions about how to accomplish that using today's technologies and materials. Each student, to show what he knows, writes a short script about his topic, weaving facts in with original ideas.

Learn Transferable Skills

Gluing sugar cubes into the shape of an igloo is not a skill students are likely to use again. In addition to integrating higher-level thinking into the Synthesis step, students should also gain transferable skills as they are producing results. These skills include:

- Writing (composing)
- Technology
- Presentation
- Production (e.g., poster, video, model)
- Performance

Of course, you do not need to include all skills every time, but a combination can be effective. However, consider including a composition (letter, essay, higher-level report, story) each time students engage in the information search process. When each student produces a composition, you can assess specifically what that student gained from the experience, along with providing opportunities for students to write in various subject areas. Students can complete group projects concurrently with the individually written paper, using many forms of creative expression resulting in a presentation, performance, or production using a variety of technology applications as appropriate.

Collaborating with teachers in other subject areas and the technology department adds another dimension to the learning; students see a dynamic team of experts working together on their behalf. The library media specialist, homeroom teacher, language arts, fine arts, and technology specialists planning and teaching in tandem, for example, integrate a number of transferable skills taught at a level any one teacher may not be able to reach alone.

Compiling a bibliography, whether or not the student speaks, constructs, performs, or composes the final product, teaches an additional transferable skill. See Chapter Nine for suggestions on citing sources for middle school students. If students cite sources in the Use of Information step, they can easily put them in alphabetical order for the bibliography.

Provide an Audience

Let's face it—performing in front of an audience raises our level of concern and increases the amount of effort we put forth. Students will take more pride in work that will be viewed by many eyes, even if the "eyes" are imaginary, such as those in the example of the sixth graders' city council presentations and the ninth graders' consultation with the movie producer. Or, knowing that the library will display their projects, students understand that any library visitor will view their work. You get the idea; stated audience = better results.

By combining information found in sources, original ideas and higher-level thought, and transferable skills in the Synthesis step of Big6, students will produce meaningful results.

Get Started

Introduce Synthesis to Students: Plan

Considering the following points can make planning for Synthesis quite manageable:

What product or products will best show the results of the information search? Often the nature of the information problem (see Chapter Six) will indicate how students will show results, such as the "lessons," that the class will write for the State Office of Immigrant Education or a rock cycle display that elementary students can understand. Most often the results of information searching can take on a variety of formats. What instruction and practice do students need to create the product or performance?

Big6 #5.1: Organize Information from Multiple Sources

How will students organize information from a variety of sources? Not only should the information found through research be processed at a higher level as often as possible, but how will students add original thought? Possible formats for organizing information may include diagrams, outlines, storyboards, rough drafts, sketches, and graphic organizers (see additional strategies in this chapter). What training do students need to create these organizers?

Big6 #5.2: Present the Result

Consider which transferable skills students will learn as they add value to the final product. Middle school students can effectively collaborate on group products; however, each student should also provide evidence of his or her knowledge through writing compositions such as stories or reports that include information from consulting sources as well as evidence of higher-level thought.

Most state curriculum standards include using technology to show the results of an information search process or inquiry. If the nature of the final product allows meaningful use of technology, how can students effectively use the available technological resources to show results of information searching? What instruction do students need in using specific technology? Who will provide the instruction? Do you need to reserve a lab or laptop cart for several days in a row?

How will students give credit to sources cited in Use of Information? Will you require students to use a standard such as Modern Language Association (MLA) to create a bibliography? What instruction do students need to create a list of sources used? Allowing students to use an online service such as David Warlick's Citation Machine <http://citationmachine.net> still requires that they identify the components of the intellectual property, but takes the tedium out of formatting the citation for the bibliography. While free citation services do not include all formats, they include those that middle school students will most likely use, such as books, encyclopedias, free Web sites, and subscription databases. Teachers must require students to give credit to sources from which they used information, as this is the first defense against plagiarism.

Deliver Instruction

Display the Big6 chart and direct students' attention to Big6 #5.1: Organize Information from Multiple Sources and #5.2 Present Results. Instruct or review with students how to organize the information they found, including any original ideas they will offer for the results.

Teach students how to put information together for presenting results by modeling the process. Especially note any application, analysis, synthesis, or evaluation that needs to be performed on the information, as these higher-level skills remain elusive for many middle school learners because their cognitive development has not matured into abstract levels. However, students whose cognitive development hovers between the concrete operational and the formal operational levels can offer original ideas and respond to questions that require divergent and evaluative thinking.

Finally, teach or review the transferable technology, writing, performance, presentation, or production skills needed for the final products.

Additional Strategies for Engaging Students in Synthesis

Copyright

The concept of intellectual property is "beyond the radar" of middle school students. Teachers and library media specialists need to teach the definition of intellectual property and what it covers, as well as the laws that protect it, in order for students to appreciate the idea of property that is not tangible in the same way as an MP3 player or a guitar. Students (and many adults) think that if they can access information for free then they can use it freely. Yes, as long as students are not publicly displaying copyrighted material, they have more freedom in how they use information for academic purposes than do teachers. However, students must abide by copyright laws and guidelines in order to appreciate the efforts put forth by the original authors and copyright owners. Teach your students about the reason they must cite sources and get permissions for certain uses of copyrighted material. Ask students to name a favorite thing they own. How would they feel if someone stole it? How would they feel if someone else copied or published a story or song that they wrote?

Listing and explaining copyright laws and guidelines is beyond the scope of this text. One of the best books on copyright in the K-12 environment is by Carol Simpson, who has years of experience and vast expertise in the field. (Simpson, Carol. Copyright for Schools: A Practical Guide. 4th Ed. Worthington, OH: Linworth Books, 2005. ISBN 1-58683-192-5.)

Teach Students to Avoid Plagiarism

Articulating the definition of plagiarism and stating expectations to children goes a long way in preventing it. Discuss the concept of plagiarism with students, underscoring the importance of students valuing their own work and original ideas. In their two groundbreaking books about plagiarism, Ann Lathrop and Kathleen Foss provide educators with valuable ideas and strategies.

- Lathrop, Ann and Kathleen Foss. *Student Cheating and Plagiarism in the Internet Era: A Wake-Up Call.* Englewood, Colorado: Libraries Unlimited, 2000.

- Lathrop, Ann and Kathleen Foss. *Guiding Students from Cheating and Plagiarism to Honesty and Integrity: Strategies for Change.* Westport, Connecticut.: Libraries Unlimited, 2005.

Also consider posting a statement about plagiarism on your school's or library's Web site (Figure 10.2) or on a poster in the school library media center so that students and parents understand the school's stand on this growing issue.

Practice Tested Reading and Writing Skills

Writing fictional stories or historical fiction based on the facts found in the information search process provides meaningful practice for many states' tested reading and writing skills. Students can work through the writing process as the Synthesis phase of the Big6 process (see Part III: The Big6 Writing Process Organizers). Language arts teachers can require students to include one or more of the following reading skills into their story:

- cause and effect relationships
- problem and solution
- compare and contrast
- characters' opinions
- logical sequence
- generalizations
- logical conclusions

Once stories are edited, revised, and published, students can read each others' stories, identifying and discussing any of the above components. Collaboration between social studies or science teachers and language arts teachers will bring the expertise of the subject area and the reading and writing teachers together for the benefit of the students. In addition, writing stories may be a refreshing change of pace from the traditional written report that is usually the result most students expect to produce from their information search.

Include an About the Author Section

Using a digital camera, students can include with their final product a portrait and short biography. Condensing their life into a few sentences also gives an opportunity to practice summarizing. As with a published author, they can include other works, awards, and accomplishments in which they take pride. Exercise caution when displaying student work in public—they should not reveal personal information.

Create Original Illustrations

Instead of overusing clip art, have students create their own illustrations using electronic paint programs, digital cameras, or illustration tools such as paint or markers. If a scanner is available, students can scan their original art for inclusion in a paper, story, or other electronic publishing method.

Statement on Plagiarism
School Name Here

What is plagiarism? Presenting someone else's ideas as your own, not giving credit to sources that you use in any type of written or oral assignment, and purchasing papers off the Web or having someone else write one for you is considered plagiarism. This is academic dishonesty and those who practice it are subject to disciplinary actions by the school's administration.

Why do some students plagiarize? Sometimes students do not realize that they have to give credit to a source when they summarize or paraphrase someone else's ideas. Or, they may be afraid that their own ideas are not worthy. Some students may procrastinate on an assignment and not have time to compose original ideas, being forced to cheat to get the assignment in on time. The subject matter of the assignment may be uninteresting and a student chooses to copy from someone else instead of learning it for himself. Occasionally, a student may lack integrity and behave dishonestly in various aspects of his or her life, including cheating on schoolwork. Whatever the reason, plagiarism is dishonest and must be avoided.

How can you avoid plagiarizing?

1. Set a timeline for completing assignments so that you have adequate time to complete research, process information, and present original thinking.

2. Give proper credit when you use ideas that you obtained from sources other than yourself, even when you summarize or paraphrase them in your own words. You can get citation guidelines in the library or from your teacher.

3. If you are unsure whether or not you may be plagiarizing, check with your librarian or teacher for help.

4. If you don't understand an assignment, or just don't want to do it, talk to your teacher about it instead of cheating and copying from someone else.

5. Consider the disservice you are doing yourself by not learning from the body of knowledge or contributing original ideas to it.

Think Before Using PowerPoint as Presentation Tool

Some call them "PowerPoint-less" presentations. We all have witnessed and graded those student presentations featuring PowerPoint—not as a visual support to a thoughtfully delivered oral presentation, but merely to show off the bells and whistles of the software. PowerPoint, as well as other presentation packages, has the "power" to allow students to create visuals for carefully crafted, higher-level presentations, as it keeps their audience focused. It also has the potential to let students use it to deliver superficial oral reports that are nothing more than the child reading from bulleted texts as words swirl across the slide, distracting the audience from the intended content. Figure 10.3 shows a series of slides constructed by a sixth grader for a unit on Ancient Egypt. The child simply read the words on the slides, never elaborating on the content or taking her eyes off the text.

Figure 10.3: Poorly Constructed PowerPoint Slides and Presentation

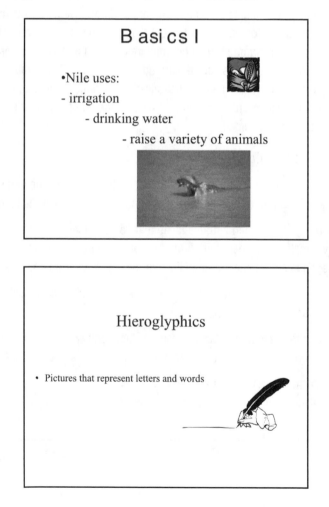

Hieroglyphics

- The Egyptian type of writing

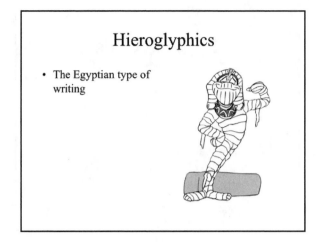

Appearance

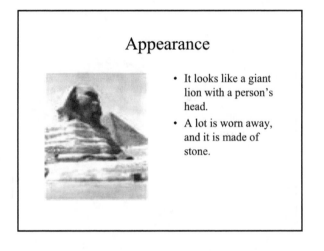

- It looks like a giant lion with a person's head.
- A lot is worn away, and it is made of stone.

The Sphinx

- The sphinx is a monument in Egypt made by the ancient Egyptians

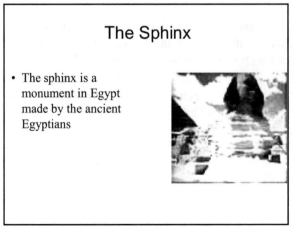

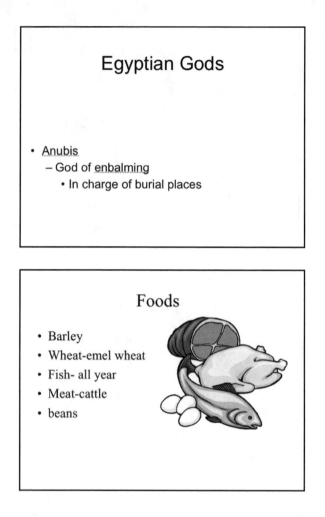

Egyptian Gods

- Anubis
  - God of enbalming
    - In charge of burial places

Foods

- Barley
- Wheat-emel wheat
- Fish- all year
- Meat-cattle
- beans

The teacher should consider whether or not PowerPoint is the best means to show the results of the research and thinking. If so, then students must have strict guidelines (of course, allowing for creativity) from which to construct their slides and orally present the results. Students need to know that PowerPoint itself is not the presentation, it is merely the visual that supports the content and helps the audience stay focused. The PowerPoint slides are the "table of contents" for the "chapters" that student will present.

PowerPoint Slide Show Guidelines for Students

Before you create a PowerPoint slide show, ask yourself this question: "Is this the best format to aid in presenting the results of my research findings and conclusions?" If you answer "yes," consider the following criteria when creating your slide show:

- [ ] Begin with an introductory slide including your topic and the names of the presenters.
- [ ] Each slide should contain main points, not the entire text of your presentation. You should use the points for elaboration. Give your classmates a reason to have to listen to you and take notes if needed.
- [ ] Font size should be no smaller than 32 points and the style should be consistent throughout the slide show.
- [ ] Font color should contrast with the background color. Font color, typeface, and contrast should be visible. You should not have to turn off the lights to read your slides.
- [ ] Text animation should be used sparingly, if at all. Use it to make a point, not to entertain. Overuse of animation will distract your audience.
- [ ] Images should reinforce or extend the content and be visible from the back of the room. Be careful—text may be difficult to read if superimposed over graphics.
- [ ] Use a lot of "white space," refraining from cluttering each slide.
- [ ] Use sound prudently—only for extending or supporting the content.
- [ ] Slide transitions should be consistent throughout the presentation.
- [ ] If linking to Web sites, the Web pages should also be visible from the back of the room.
- [ ] Use correct grammar, spelling, punctuation, and capitalization.
- [ ] Include a "Works Cited" slide, giving credit to the sources of information you used.
- [ ] Include an opening slide stating that your project contains copyrighted materials (if indeed it does), which have been used under the fair use exemption of the U.S. Copyright Law. If you have made alterations, those must be indicated.

Use a Wiki to Support Synthesis

See Chapter Six for introduction to using wikis.

Project wiki: Provide detailed directions for organizing information from all sources and for creating the final product (Figure 10.4). Include transferable skills and higher-level thinking components. Direct students' attention to any scoring guides that may be uploaded to the Evaluation page, so that they can meet the stated expectations as they make their final products.

Group wikis: Each group may use its Synthesis pages for organizing information and making notes on how they plan to produce the final product. The wiki itself will not act as the final product, only as a way to organize it.

Figure 10.4: Project Wiki: Synthesis

Big6 Wiki Project | Synthesis

Home   Discuss   Changes   All Pages   Log In to Edit   search here

Your group needs to create a lesson for your (imaginary) class of immigrants. It will teach the basic concepts of your topic. You should also show them how this concept will be of benefit to them as newcomers to the state. You need to create a study sheet on which they can take notes. Your classmates will act as the immigrants, using your study sheet to take notes for a quiz in which everyone will be responsible.

You may use Power Point if you use it effectively. Information on the slides should be the "table of contents" for your presentation. You should elaborate on the points on the slides, not just read from them word for word.

You do not have to use Power Point. Be creative in your ideas. You will need to engage and keep the attention of the class. Remember, this content has the potential to be boring. Don't put your class to sleep!

You must have your plan outlined before presenting your idea to Ms. Jones for approval. Use your wiki to create your group's outline.

All presentations will be graded based on our Presentation Guidelines which are attached to this file.

Big6 copyright Michael Eisenberg and Robert Berkowitz, 1987. Big6 Wiki Project pages created by Barbara A. Jansen, 2005.

SideBar

Big6 Skills

Task Definition
Information Seeking Strategies
Location and Access
Use of Information
Synthesis
Evaluation

Research Journal

Big6 copyright Eisenberg and Berkowitz, 1987. Big6 Wiki Project created by Barbara A. Jansen, 2005.

Specific Uses of Technology to Support Synthesis

Figure 10.5: Possible Uses of Technology in Synthesis

Synthesis	Possible technologies used
5.1 Organize information from	Class project: Use the project wiki (see Chapter Six for introduction to wikis) to describe the method in which each group should organize their information. Students use the Synthesis page on their group wikis for organizing the information for their final product. Students, in groups or individually, use the outlining feature in a word processor or PowerPoint to organize information. Electronic graphic organizers such as Inspiration™ Software <http://www.inspiration.com> help students organize and to make connections between ideas.
5.2 Present results	Word processing: stories, essays, reports, bibliography. Illustration and photo editing: create and insert graphics and photos into word processed compositions and PowerPoint presentations. Web authoring: create Web pages. Podcasts, Web logs (blogs), video logs (vlogs). Use digital cameras, video recorders, scanners to create DVD and videos. Multimedia. Spreadsheet, database, timelines. Charts and graphs, tables.

Chapter 11

Evaluation

W e often neglect the final step of the Big6 process—evaluation. So far, students have completed the information search, given presentations, turned in projects and papers, and teachers have recorded grades—now on to the next topic!

Wait! How will students gain proficiency in internalizing the steps of the information search process? How will students identify the skills within the process in which they are efficient or need additional practice? How will students determine their level of success or areas needing improvement? They learn evaluation skills through the practice of self-evaluation.

What does evaluation mean in Big6 terms? Not to be confused with assessment—grades given by teachers—evaluation is the process by which students identify their own strengths and weaknesses. A higher-level thought process in itself, middle school students can still successfully accomplish this step with guidance and deliberate, age-appropriate questions posed by their library media specialists and teachers.

Evaluate Process and Product

Students must have the opportunity to evaluate their efforts before turning in final products or delivering presentations. Too often students are content to turn in a first draft of a product. By having students evaluate before turning in assignments, they can fix problems and will gain awareness that research is a multi-step, recursive process. They will understand that revisiting completed steps and making revisions is possible and highly encouraged!

Formal Self-Evaluation Guide

Providing two types of evaluation instruments will encourage students to put forth their best effort and produce work of which they and you can be proud. The first evaluation instrument students should receive is the scoring rubric (Figure 11.1), guide, or checklist that you will use to assess their work and assign a grade. By demystifying the expectations of the assignment, you will encourage students to rise to your standards.

Middle school students can occasionally have a voice in the scoring criteria, giving them greater buy-in and reason to expend more effort toward the final results. A free tool for generating rubrics is available at <http://rubistar.4teachers.org>. Below is an abbreviated example for a sixth grade scoring rubric:

Figure 11.1: Abbreviated Example of Scoring Rubric

	Beginning 1	Developing 2	Accomplished 3	Exemplary 4	Score
Note taking	Minimal notes turned in, no sources noted, disorganized	Adequate notes taken, few sources noted, somewhat organized	Notes taken, sources noted on most, organized	Thorough notes taken, sources noted on each, well-organized	
Written paper	Paper unorganized, no original ideas, poorly written, missing bibliography, much too short or long	Paper somewhat organized, some original ideas, adequately written, bibliography included, within correct length	Paper organized and adequately written with adequate original ideas, bibliography included, correct length	Paper well-organized and thoughtfully presented, containing many original ideas, about 250 words, bibliography included in proper MLA style	

You can also provide content and process checklists for students to use, if you are unable to create a scoring instrument. Checklists will direct students to judge the quality of their results and give them opportunities to revise before turning in the work. You will find examples of content and process checklists at the end of this chapter.

Informal Self-Evaluation Guide

The second type of self-evaluation is a less formal set of directed, developmentally appropriate questions to which students will respond in writing. These questions relate to students' perceptions about experiences with the information and in working with others. Having to articulate ideas in written form will ensure that the student think deeply and make connections that otherwise would be lost in the process. Teachers and library media specialists can easily determine the benefits and less desirable outcomes of the assignment and gather evidence of affective behaviors, such as attitudes towards learning and cooperative work, which would otherwise be difficult to assess. Require students to submit the written evaluation along with notes and final result. You may wish to only assess a grade for effort and completion instead of judging responses, because the answers are purely subjective.

Students can answer questions such as: What did I learn? What did I learn how to do that I can use again? How can I use it? What did I do well on my project? What could I do better next time? Did I include the information I found out about my subject? Which sources did I find useful? Which sources did I need but did not have? What did I contribute to my group? What did I like most about doing this project? I think my grade will be _____ because... These guides are easily created using word processing software. Allow plenty of room for students to narrate and adequate time for completing the questions.

Give Students Early Access to Self-Evaluation Guides

In order for students to know early in the process the expectations of the assignment and the information-seeking behaviors, give students the scoring and self-evaluation instruments soon after discussing the Task Definition. If the final product is introduced after the note-gathering step, provide the scoring guide and self-evaluation before students begin to work on it so that students have the standard by which to judge their results. Allow (and encourage) students to revisit steps of the Big6 to fix any deficiency before turning in their final work.

The teachers and library media specialist who collaborated on the assignment should read the evaluations to determine effective strategies and those needing modification for the next information search activity. Students also articulate affective behaviors through this written opportunity:

- "I learned a lot about group work. I found that I can't always have my way, and that if I couldn't say something appropriate, it's best to keep my mouth shut."

- "I learned that working in a group is better than working alone because the work is more spread out."

- "Next time I do this, I won't play around as much as I did, and I'll take more notes."

- "I think what I could do differently next time is to make a better conclusion and try not to fidget so much."

- "I learned that it takes a lot of cooperation—that one person can't do it all or things don't get done."

- "I learned that groups of people won't pick your idea unless you explain it very well."

- "Next time we do something like this, I will try to be here more often to actually know exactly what my group is doing! And try not to be so bossy!"

- "Working with people for a long time can sometimes be frustrating. You have to know how to work together."

- "Compensation—you give a little and take a little."

Get Started

Introduce Evaluation Strategies to Students: Plan

Big6 #6.1: Judge the Result and Big6 #6.2: Judge the Process

Begin by preparing the scoring guide, checklist, or rubric that you will use to assess student performance. Next, create the informal self-evaluation guide for students to use during the completion of the information search process. Make sure you have enough copies of both for each student. Unlike other steps of the process, Evaluation is best completed independently, ensuring that each student reflects on and articulates his own efforts and experiences.

Deliver Instruction

Formal Self-Evaluation Guide

Sometime before students begin to search independently for information, preferably soon after the Task Definition phase of instruction, inform students that you are providing them with the same scoring guide that you will be using to assess their work. Tell them that this is part of Big6 #6: Evaluation, but that you are giving it to them at this time so that they can work toward the expectations from the beginning and have no surprises at the end of the process.

Informal Self-Evaluation Guide

After students have completed Big6 #5: Synthesis and submitted their final work, including their evaluation based on the formal evaluation guide, direct the class to the Big6 chart or poster and focus on the last step: Evaluation. Discuss the importance of "thinking about their thinking and learning." Tell students to take time to reflect and give you feedback on their efforts and on the information search experience. Tell them that you will read their comments and use them to modify the process for the next project. They should be honest and candid. Students need at least 15 minutes to complete the informal evaluation, and it is best done in the structure and quiet of the classroom instead of assigned as homework.

Additional Strategies for Engaging Students in Evaluation

Evaluate Progress

Continuous evaluation can and should occur during each step of the Big6 search process. Upon completion of the search process each day, consider leaving 5 to 10 minutes for students to write in a research journal (Figure 11.2). They can respond to prompts such as the ones below:

Figure 11.2: Research Journal

Research Journal

Name: _____

Date: _____

Information researched:

(Respond to the checked questions)

☐ What did I learn today?

☐ What did I learn about how I search for or use information?

☐ On what do I need to ask for help tomorrow?

☐ Who should I ask?

☐ Which step of the Big6 process did I work on today?

☐ Did I finish that step?

☐ Where do I start tomorrow?

☐ What source will I use?

☐ How well did I stay focused today?

☐ If I had a hard time focusing, what caused my distractions?

☐ What can I do so that I am not distracted tomorrow?

Of course, students will not answer all of the above questions each day. Pose a few selected questions to the class or give certain students questions that focus on their particular needs. Students can check the questions required for the day. If possible, ongoing evaluation can, and should, be tailored to fit the learning styles and intellectual requirements of each student. By reflecting on the day's efforts, students articulate their progress and begin recognizing strengths and weaknesses in their individual search process. At the beginning of the class period the next day, have students look at their journal entry from the day before so they know where to start and how to avoid distraction.

Group Evaluation

Name: _____ **Class period:** _____

1. Explain your contribution to the group's effort. (What did you contribute?)

Circle the points you should receive   1   2   3   4

2. Explain_____'s contribution to the group's effort.

Circle the points this group member should receive   1   2   3   4

3. Explain_____'s contribution to the group's effort.

Circle the points this group member should receive   1   2   3   4

4. What did you find satisfying about doing this project?

5. What would you change if you were designing this project?

6. Did you have enough time to complete the project? ____ yes   ____ no

Peer Evaluation

When working in groups, some middle school students have the potential to play around. Usually, the Big6 experience—especially if prefaced with an engaging information problem and questions—works to motivate and settle them down. However, there may be those few who will want to edge by with as little work as possible. Knowing that their peers, as well as you, will evaluate their efforts should help keep them focused. Peer evaluation (Figure 11.3) should be taken for what it is: middle school students judging middle school students! However, it can serve as a powerful insight into the relationships and chemistry of students working together. Tell the groups that they will evaluate each other based on each group member's efforts and contributions to the project. The evaluations should be honest and will not be seen by the other members of the group. During the informal self-evaluation phase of the process, allow students to evaluate the project as well as each other.

Use a Wiki to Support Evaluation

See Chapter Six for introduction to using wikis.

Project wiki: Post instructions for completing ongoing and final evaluation (Figure 11.4). Students can access the file you uploaded to the project wiki. You will want them to complete a formal and an informal evaluation. Consider having students evaluate the project and the efforts of their teammates.

Group wikis: Each group member can add to his Evaluation page the evaluation of the project, based on the questions you provided. He can complete the formal and informal evaluation in writing, or by copying and pasting it to a word processor.

Figure 11.4: Project Wiki: Evaluation

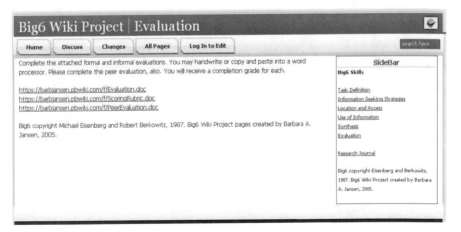

Specific Uses of Technology to Support Evaluation

Figure 11.5: Possible Uses of Technology in Evaluation

Evaluation	Possible technologies used
1.1 Judge the result (effectiveness)	Provide students with an online version of the scoring guide the teacher will use for grading, or have the content checklist available on the school's server for students to access and submit.
1.2 Judge the process (efficiency)	Make available the informal self-evaluation guide in electronic format for students to access. Use blogs, wikis, or journaling services for encouraging students to keep a research journal. Use the project wiki to post evaluations. Students use their group wiki to access and respond to group evaluation.

Examples of Content Checklists

The wording on these guides should be changed to meet the specific requirements of the assignment and needs of the students.

Evaluate Your Research Skills using the Big6™

By Barbara A. Jansen and Robert E. Berkowitz

Name: _____ Date: _____

Before you turn in your assignment or project, think about and respond to the items.

Big6 #1: Task Definition	☐ Does the information in your final product meet (or exceed) the requirements of the assignment? ☐ Does your final product meet your teacher's expectations?
Big6 #2: Information Seeking Strategies	☐ Did the books, Web sites, and other resources you used meet the needs of the assignment? ☐ Did you select the best sources available to you? How do you know?
Big6 #3: Location & Access	☐ Did you locate the sources you needed? ☐ Did you find the information you needed in each source?
Big6 #4: Use of Information	☐ Were you able to effectively identify the information you needed? ☐ Were you able to effectively take notes or gather information?
Big6 #5: Synthesis	☐ Did you effectively organize information? ☐ Does your product present the information clearly?
Big6 #6: Evaluation	☐ Does your product meet (or exceed) the assignment requirements? ☐ Did you use your time well?

Figure 11.7: Evaluating an Assignment

Checklist for Completing an Assignment

How will you know you have done your best on a school assignment?
Before you turn in an assignment to your teacher, make sure it is as perfect as possible. You should be proud to put your name on the assignment.

Name: _____ Date: _____

You should be able to answer "yes" to all of these questions before you turn in your assignment. If you answer "no" to any of these questions, revise your assignment before you turn it in.

Is what I created to finish the assignment what my teacher wants me to do?
____ yes ____ no

Did I include all the information required for the assignment?
____ yes ____ no

Do the results of my efforts reflect my original ideas or my own work?
____ yes ____ no

Did I give credit to all my sources, even if my teacher did not require me to do so?
____ yes ____ no

Is my work neat?
____ yes ____ no

Is my work complete and includes heading information such as my name and the date?
____ yes ____ no

Would I be proud for anyone to look at my work?
____ yes ____ no

Figure 11.8: Evaluating a Science Fair Project

Checklist for Completing a Science Fair Project

Name: _____ **Date:** _____

Before you take your project to school or to the science fair, answer the following questions to make sure that you have done your best work:

1. Evaluate your method.

Was the method the best way to prove or disprove the hypothesis?
___ yes ___ no

If you answered "no," then what would you change about the method? Add this to your conclusion.

2. Evaluate your background research.

Did your background research give you adequate information about your subject to help you start planning your experiment? ___ yes ___ no

If not, what information should you have researched?

Is it too late to add this information to your report? ___ yes ___ no

3. Evaluate your display.

Does your display contain your name and a title? ___ yes ___ no

Is the displayed text word processed, neat, and organized using headings and subheadings? ___ yes ___ no

Do the text, graphics, and photographs help the judges and audience understand your process and results? ___ yes ___ no

Are your materials dangerous? ___ yes ___ no

Can your materials break or spill and harm young children who may look at your project?___ yes ___ no

If you answered "yes," what can you do to prevent an injury?
This is very important!

Would you be proud for anyone to view this project?___ yes ___ no

Checklist for a Writing Assignment
Grades 5-6

Name: _____ **Date:** _____

Before you show your paper to others, make sure it is as perfect as possible. You should be proud to put your name on your paper.

You should be able to answer "yes" to all of these questions before you turn in your paper:

Did you do everything in the assignment and include all that was required for the paper? ____ yes ____ no

Does your final paper show your original ideas as well as other information you found? ____ yes ____ no

Did you give credit to all of your sources in a list (bibliography) at the end of your paper? ____ yes ____ no

Is your paper word processed (or very neatly typed or hand-written if you do not have access to a computer)? ____ yes ____ no

Is your paper complete and does it include a title page with heading information (title, your name, your teacher's name, date)? ____ yes ____ no

If your teacher asks for these, did you include your notes, copies of each version, and your list of books, people, and Web sites? ____ yes ____ no

Would you be proud for anyone to read this paper? ____ yes ____ no

Checklist for a Writing Assignment
Grades 7-9

Name: _____ Date: _____

You should be able to answer "yes" to all of these questions before you turn in your paper:

Is your final paper a thoughtful response to the assignment? ___ yes ___ no

Does your final paper represent your ideas and conclusions? ___ yes ___ no

Is your paper more than just a summary of other people's ideas?
___ yes ___ no

If you paraphrased or summarized information found in books or magazines, on the Internet, or from other people, did you cite the source at point of use in your paper (using a footnote or parenthetical reference)?
___ yes ___ no

Did you give credit to all of your sources in a bibliography? ___ yes ___ no

Did you do everything in the assignment? ___ yes ___ no

Does your bibliography follow the MLA format? Find out if your teacher requires a format other than MLA. ___ yes ___ no

Is your paper word processed (or very neatly typed or handwritten if you do not have access to a computer)? ___ yes ___ no

Is your paper complete and does it include a title page with heading information (title, your name, your teacher's name, date)? ___ yes ___ no

If your teacher requests these, did you include your notes, copies of each draft, and an annotated bibliography? ___ yes ___ no

Would you be proud for anyone to read this paper? ___ yes ___ no

Chapter 12

Putting It All Together

Correlating the Big6 to State Curriculum Standards and Tested Skills

Integrating the Big6 within subject-area content satisfies multiple state-mandated curriculum standards, including many that are tested yearly on high-stakes exams. Consider the objectives that are taught when students are writing and using technology within the regular curriculum in English language arts (reading and writing), math, social studies, science, health, foreign language, or other subjects. Correlating the Big6 process and individual steps with your state's prescribed curriculum standards and skills tested on the state's high stakes annual performance exam proves that when students engage in the Big6 process they are doing so in a meaningful way. By the very nature of the process, students are interacting with content and skills standards and practicing those tested skills in a meaningful and authentic manner, instead of merely filling out practice worksheets. Below you will find a correlation of the Big6 Skills and the Texas Assessment of Knowledge and Skills for social studies, tested at grade eight (Figure 12.1) and a correlation of Big6 Skills and The Texas Essential Knowledge and Skills for a portion of English Language Arts for grade six (Figure 12.2) to use as a model for correlating the Big6 with your state's academic standards.

Correlation Between Big6™ Skills and Texas Assessment of Knowledge & Skills (the state's exam)

Big6 #6: Skill	TAKS Social Studies Objectives
	Grade Eight
The entire Big6™ process can be used to support the mastery of all history; government, geography; economics; culture; science; technology, and society; and citizenship objectives in social studies	**All content objectives:** history; government; geography; economics; culture; science, technology, and society; and citizenship
#2.1 Identify possible source #2.2 Choose best sources #3.1 Locate sources #3.2 Access information within sources #4.1 Engage in sources #4.2 Extract relevant information	**The student will use critical thinking skills to analyze social studies information.** (8.30) **Social studies skills.** The student applies critical-thinking skills to organize and use information acquired from a variety of sources including electronic technology. The student is expected to (A) [differentiate between, locate, and] use primary and secondary sources [such as computer software, databases, media and news services, biographies, interviews, and artifacts] to acquire information about the United States
#4.1 Engage in sources #4.2 Extract relevant information	(B) analyze information by sequencing, categorizing, identifying cause-and-effect relationships, comparing, contrasting, finding the main idea, summarizing, making generalizations [and predictions], and drawing references and conclusions
#5.1 Organize information from multiple sources #5.2 Present results	(C) [organize and] interpret information from [outlines, reports, databases, and] visuals including graphs, charts, timelines, and maps
#4.1 Engage in sources	(D) identify points of view from the historical context surrounding an event and the frame of reference which influence the participants
#4.1 Engage in sources	(E) identity bias in written, [oral,] and visual material

Correlation Between Big6™ Skills and Texas Essential Knowledge & Skills for English Language Arts

(state curriculum standards for grade six)

Big6 #6: Skill	TEKS English Language Arts Objectives (partial)
	Grade Six
1.2 Identify the information needed	(6.13) The student is expected to (A) form and revise questions for investigations, including questions arising from readings, assignments, and units of study.
3.2 Find information within source 4.1 Engage in sources	(B) Use text organizers, including headings, graphic features, and tables of contents, to locate and organize information.
4.1 Engage in sources 4.2 Extract relevant information	(C) Use multiple sources, including electronic texts, experts, and print resources, to locate information relevant to research questions.
4.1 Engage in sources 4.2 Extract relevant information	(D) Interpret and use graphic sources of information such as maps, graphs, timelines, or tables to address research questions.
4.2 Extract relevant information 5.1 Organize information from multiple sources	(E) Summarize and organize information from multiple sources by taking notes, outlining ideas, and making charts.
5.2 Present results	(F) Produce research projects and reports in effective formats for various audiences.
5.1 Organize information from multiple sources 5.2 Present results	(G) Draw conclusions from information gathered from multiple sources.
1.2 Identify the information needed	(H) Use compiled information and knowledge to raise additional, unanswered questions.
5.2 Present results	(I) Present organized statements, reports, and speeches using visuals or media to support meaning as appropriate.

The blank correlation documents (Figures 12.3, 12.4, and 12.5) will help you get started on making your own correlation. Library media specialists will want to complete these for all grades and subjects, helping them justify to teachers and administrators, the importance of integrated information and technology skills within the framework of the Big6. The correlations prove that Big6 is not an "add-on" to the curriculum, but an integral part of it that is included in the state's exams and curriculum standards. Create similar blank word processing tables for other subject areas such as math, foreign language, health, career options, physical education, and fine arts.

Correlation Between Big6™ Skills
and State Curriculum Standards or Tested Skills

Big6 #6: Skill	Social Studies Objectives
	Grade(s):
The entire Big6™ process can be used to support the mastery of all history; government, geography; economics; culture; science, technology, and society; and citizenship objectives in social studies.	**All content objectives:** history; government; geography; economics; culture; science, technology, and society; and citizenship
Big6 Skill(s)	Curriculum standard or tested skills:
Big6 Skill(s)	Curriculum standard or tested skills:
Big6 Skill(s)	Curriculum standard or tested skills:
Big6 Skill(s)	Curriculum standard or tested skills:
Big6 Skill(s)	Curriculum standard or tested skills:

Correlation Between Big6 Skills
and State Curriculum Standards or Tested Skills

Big6 #6: Skill	Language Arts Objectives
	Grade(s):
Big6 Skill(s)	Curriculum standard or tested skills:
Big6 Skill(s)	Curriculum standard or tested skills:
Big6 Skill(s)	Curriculum standard or tested skills:
Big6 Skill(s)	Curriculum standard or tested skills:
Big6 Skill(s)	Curriculum standard or tested skills:
Big6 Skill(s)	Curriculum standard or tested skills:

Correlation Between Big6™ Skills
and State Curriculum Standards or Tested Skills

Big6 #6: Skill	Science Objectives
	Grade(s):
The entire Big6™ process can be used to support the mastery of all history; government, geography; economics; culture; science, technology, and society; and citizenship content objectives in science.	**All content objectives:** general, life, and earth science, such as, human body systems, solar system, cell structure, rock cycle
Big6 Skill(s)	Curriculum standard or tested skills:
Big6 Skill(s)	Curriculum standard or tested skills:
Big6 Skill(s)	Curriculum standard or tested skills:
Big6 Skill(s)	Curriculum standard or tested skills:
Big6 Skill(s)	Curriculum standard or tested skills:

Integrate the Big6 in Content Areas: Lesson Plans

In the lesson plans that follow, specific curriculum standards are not included, due to the variations in wording from state to state. Of course, teachers should use these plans as guides for designing instruction, modifying to meet the requirements of their subject-area state prescribed curriculum and the cognitive levels of their students. The plans indicate a grade level only as a guide for the developmental appropriateness of the information skills activities, not necessarily for the content covered, as curriculum varies across grades from state to state.

The time estimate is just that—an estimate. The time will vary for each class's level of experience with each step of Big6 and skills within the steps, and for modifications made in the plan. In addition, some elements of a lesson may be written into a plan, such as a scoring rubric, but may not actually be included. Of course, teachers who modify these plans for their state or district curriculum will create the missing pieces to complete the plan for their students.

These lessons are for demonstration purposes only. You will want to take ideas from them, explore other approaches and possibilities, and adapt the content to your program's and students' needs. Consideration must be taken into account and accommodations made for students who have learning or language challenges.

Each lesson assumes that the classroom teacher, library media specialist, and technology teacher (if applicable) will collaborate to plan and teach his or her area of expertise. See Collaboration Strategies in Part III for ideas on responsibilities of the teacher and library media specialist in lesson planning and instructional delivery.

Grade: Five

Content objectives: Reading—reading for information; writing process skills—specifically plot development, sequencing, and imagery; social studies history—The American Revolution

Information skill objectives: Note taking, using subscription databases

Technology skill objectives: Word processing

Time estimate: Three weeks for study of American Revolution, additional research, and writing

? **Information problem:** Ms. Mendez, our library media specialist, noticed that we do not have many short stories set in the period up to and during the American Revolution for the library collection. We have read several historical novels (list these for the students) and are about to study the American Revolution. What could we do to help?

Let's use the Big6 to help us solve her problem. We have used the Big6 several times this year. Who can remember that we used the Big6 to help us study?

(As each of the Big6 steps is discussed in the subsequent sequence, and accompanying skills taught, display the appropriate step so students maintain focus within the process.)

Big6 #1: Task Definition

#1.1 Class brainstorms ideas, finally defining the task (with teacher's help) as: Learn about the American Revolution and write a story about it.

#1.2 Assign each student to a specific event or conflict within the American Revolution on which to take notes. As the class studies events, probably from the textbook, leading up to and the war itself, students can take notes on their topics.

Possible topics to assign individual students: causes of the Revolution (colonial resistance to British imperial policies, denial of basic rights of Englishmen to American colonists, taxation without representation, The Stamp Act, taxes on tea, Boston Tea Party, Townsend Acts, Coercive Acts); major British and American figures (King George III, Benjamin Franklin, Patrick Henry, John Adams, Thomas Jefferson, George Washington, Thomas Paine, General Charles Cornwallis, and major women contributors such as Abigail Adams, Molly Pitcher, Mercy Otis Warren, and Martha Washington); First and Second Continental Congresses, writing and approving the Declaration of Independence, major battles such as Lexington and Concord.

Once you have finished the regular study of the American Revolution, have students look at their notes. The teacher should help students craft questions for which they need more information. Provide them with two or three days to obtain additional information about their topic, because the textbook will not have gone into enough detail. Begin the individual research with Big6 #2: Information Seeking Strategies. Make sure that students understand in which stage of the Big6 they are, as you take them through the process.

You may wish to provide students with the Big6 Writing Process Organizer (Part III) for Grades 5 and 6. Assist them with each stage of the process as they work their way through the organizer.

Big6 #2: Information Seeking Strategies

Tell students that they will use library books and encyclopedias, and subscription databases Thomson Gale InfoBits, SIRS® Discoverer, and World Book® Online, to gather more information about their topics, because the textbook had limited coverage.

Big6 #3: Location and Access

#3.1 Review with students how to use the library catalog to search by subject or keyword to find library books and materials. Review how to locate the electronic resources listed above.

#3.2 Review using the indexes and tables of contents in the books and shelf encyclopedias. Demonstrate the use of the electronic resources. Show students how to access information within the databases, using the simple search feature (see Chapter Eight).

Big6 #4: Use of Information

#4.1 Once the appropriate chapter or article is located, teach students how to identify essential points of access in order to find relevant sections to begin reading for details (see Chapter Nine).

#4.2 Review "trash and treasure" note taking (see Chapter Nine). Students will use a data chart, on which they have written research questions, to record notes. Allow students time to research and take notes.

Big6 #5: Synthesis

#5.1 The teacher will either (1) compile all of the students' notes for the class to use during writing, or (2) have students write a story about the topic that they researched. Model the use of imagery by reading examples from other novels so students understand how to develop this skill.

Students will begin the writing process (see the Big6 Writing Process Organizer for Grades 5–6 in Part III for more information on the writing process, if needed). Consider having students compose directly on the keyboard. They can Save As… to preserve each draft.

Students will prewrite, draft, conference (is there a plot? logical sequence? imagery?) revise, and edit their stories. They should integrate facts from their study of the American Revolution and their topic into the story, as well as develop a plot with a logical sequence, and include evidence of imagery.

#5.2 Students will publish a final draft using word processing software. Illustrate if time permits. Determine whether or not you want students to include a bibliography, because this is fiction and typically not included. If so, they should cite sources in Big6 #4 and create the final bibliography for this step. Students should also turn in notes and all drafts.

Big6 #6: Evaluation

Students will respond to these questions during the revision stage of the writing process, in order to have time to make changes:
Before you show your paper (and product) to others, be sure it is as perfect as you can make it. This story should be something on which you are proud to put your name.
Answer "yes" to all of these questions **before** you turn in your paper:

1. Did you do everything and include all that was required for the story? (Plot, sequence, imagery?) ___ yes ___ no

2. Does your final story show your original ideas as well as other information you found? ___ yes ___ no

3. Did you give credit to all of your sources, including a written bibliography, if your teacher required one? ___ yes ___ no

4. Is your story word processed and spell checked? ___ yes ___ no

5. Is your story complete and includes your name? ___ yes ___ no

6. If your teacher asks for these, did you include your notes?
___ yes ___ no

7. Would you be proud for anyone to read this paper? ___ yes ___ no

8. Do you understand each step of the Big6 and writing processes? If not, who can you ask for help? ___ yes ___ no, I will ask
_____ for help.

Assessment: Grades taken for notes, each draft, conference, and final story. Create rubric.

Lesson Plan   The Student Council's Math Problems

Grade: Six

Content objectives: math—graphing, operations, problem-solving model, math concepts to everyday experiences

Information skill objectives: focus on survey strategies

Technology skill objectives: spreadsheet—data collection, graphing, functions

Time estimate: Three or four class periods

> **?** **Information problem:** The student council wants to sell healthy snacks in the cafeteria during lunch to earn money for community service projects. It has come to our math class for help in determining which snacks will sell the best and cost the least to supply. What is our task?

Big6 #1: Task Definition

#1.1 Discuss the information problem with the class and have them help determine how to solve it. Tell the class that we will use the Big6 to lead us through the steps to solve the problem. (Display the Big6 and point to each step throughout the process.) Help them to define the task: Find out which snacks are popular and which store or price club warehouse sells them at the cheapest cost.

#1.2 In whole group, determine what we need to find out:

    a. Which snacks are the most popular with students at our school?

    b. Would students buy healthy snacks such as little bags of carrots, nutrition bars, or cheese and crackers?

    c. Do students bring money to school?

    d. If so, how much would students pay for various snacks?

    e. Who sells them for the least cost?

Big6 #2: Information Seeking Strategies

#2.1 Whole class brainstorming: How do we find out what snacks students will buy?

#2.2 Lead students to determine that surveying their classmates and schoolmates will be the best way to find out the answers to their questions. Interview students during lunch.

Big6 #3: Location and Access

Math students locate students to interview in the cafeteria during lunch.

Big6 #4: Use of Information

Prepare the instruments for data collection. Students use the instruments to collect data during the survey by interviewing as many schoolmates as they can during lunch for one or two days, recording responses.

Big6 #5: Synthesis

#5.1 Using spreadsheet software, groups set up tables and transfer the data to the appropriate columns or rows. (Demonstrate this to class.) Show the class how to manipulate the data into various types of charts and graphs, seeing if they can determine which shows graphically the best representation of the data. Using the graphs, determine which snacks will sell the best. As a class, put all data together to make a final determination of the most popular snacks, with teacher or one student manipulating the projected spreadsheet.

Put students in groups to contact stores (by phone or online) to find out prices. They will prepare a set of questions including a statement that identifies the student, project, school, and asks for the appropriate department. Students perform the math functions to find out how much one item will cost the student council. Groups compare prices from various stores and calculate, with instruction as needed, which is the least expensive per item.

#5.2 Class decides how best to present its findings to the student council. Each group turns in its raw data, tables, graphs, and final results.

Big6 #6: Evaluation

Each student completes a group evaluation (see Chapter Eleven).

Assessment: Grade groups on their effort, data, tables, graphs, and final results. Each student in the group receives the same grade, unless circumstances dictate otherwise.

State Historical Figures Write Journals and Letters

Grade: Seven

Content objectives: writing—journals and letters, writing process; literary devices—figurative language; state history—individual contributions to the state revolution during colonization, specific battles, and statehood.

Information skill objectives: subscription database use—full-text vs. subject searching, note taking

Technology skill objectives: word processing for note taking

Time estimate: Seven class periods (two for instruction, two for note taking, and three for journal and letter writing, revision, and publishing)

? **Information problem:** You are _____ (assign each student the name of a notable figure in state history). During your life, you contribute much to the state's history. Being away from home, you keep a journal—a common practice—and write letters home. What do you include in your journal? To whom would you write and about what?

Big6 #1: Task Definition
(display Big6 chart, directing students' attention to Big6 #1)

#1.1 Have students brainstorm possible tasks from the given information problem. Write "Learn about the life, times, and contributions of _____ in order to write journal entries and letters home" on Big6 chart.

#1.2 Students, in whole class discussion, develop a list of questions that they may ask about any notable figure from their state's history. Have them look carefully at the information problem to help with developing questions. Student instructions: "Create a list of questions that you will need to know in order to produce journal entries and letters home. I will give you additional questions."

Questions for students to add to their list:

1. What role did _____ play in the state's history?

2. What significant contributions did he or she make and when?

3. What events led to these contributions?

4. What issues or problems did he or she encounter?

5. Who might he or she have written?

6. What might he or she have discussed in a letter? Journal entry? How much of this information would overlap?

Big6 #2: Information Seeking Strategies (display Big6 chart, directing students' attention to Big6 #2)

#2.1 Students brainstorm a list of sources they may use for answering these questions. Display a list for students to view. Introduce the new EBSCO History Reference Center® and discuss using netTrekker® for accessing sites from free Web. Add any obvious sources students fail to add.

#2.2 Help students narrow the list by telling them they should use library books, netTrekker®, EBSCO History Reference Center®, Thomson Gale Student Resource Center Gold, and a social studies textbook. Write these on Big6 chart.

Big6 #3: Location and Access (display Big6 chart, directing students' attention to Big6 #3)

#3.1 Show students how to access the subscription databases and reserved library books.

#3.2 Discuss and demonstrate use of subject searching vs. full-text searching. Show students the difference in the databases when they search for "James Fannin" using both types of searches. Students begin locating sources.

Big6 #4: Use of Information (display Big6 chart, directing students' attention to Big6 #4)

#4.1 Explain to students how to locate essential points of access (see instructional delivery section in Chapter Nine). Students practice on a source of information in which they have located.

#4.2 Review "trash and treasure" note taking (see Chapter Nine). Allow two class periods for note taking.

Big6 #5: Synthesis (display Big6 chart, directing students' attention to Big6 #5)

#5.1 Have students organize their notes into chronological order. Students should scrutinize their notes to see if they have enough information to write four journal entries and one letter.

#5.2 Model a journal entry. Show an authentic journal if possible. Consider using the George Washington diaries, accessible in text and scanned images, from the Library of Congress American Memory collection, available at <http://memory.loc.gov/ammem/gwhtml/gwintro.html>. Discuss what would be included in a journal or diary entry, as well as in a letter: Is it all fact? Does it all have to be fact or can the author add opinions, speculations, and other original thinking? How are the facts from the students' notes written into journal entries and letters? What original thinking could students include? How can they make their "voice" authentic? Students will write entries and letters, taking their writing through the writing process (see Part III for a writing process organizer, if needed). They will turn in final drafts of the journal entries and letter. They will turn in all notes and drafts. Provide questions from Big6 #6.1.

Big6 #6: Evaluation (display Big6 chart, directing students' attention to Big6 #6)

#6.1 Students respond to these questions before turning in their written results (provide questions as they are writing their journal entries and letter so they will understand the expectations):

    a. Are your journal entries and letter a thoughtful response to the assignment? ___ yes ___ no

    b. Do your journal entries and letter represent your ideas along with the information you found about your notable person? ___ yes ___ no

    c. Are your journal entries and letter more than just a summary of your notes? ___ yes ___ no

    d. Did you give credit to all of your sources in a bibliography? ___ yes ___ no

    e. Did you do everything in the assignment? ___ yes ___ no

    f. Is your paper hand-written, as journals and letters would be at that time in history? ___ yes ___ no

    g. Did you include your notes and copies of each draft? ___ yes ___ no

    h. Would you be proud for anyone to read your work? ___ yes ___ no

#6.2 Students complete the informal self-evaluation by answering the following questions:

- What did I learn?
- What did I learn how to do that I can use again?
- How can I use it?
- What did I do well on my project?
- What could I do better next time?
- Which sources did I find useful?
- Which sources did I need but did not have?
- What did I like most about doing this project?
- I think my grade will be _____ because…

Assessment: Scoring rubric for notes, journal entries, and letter.

Think Globally, Act Locally:
Lesson Plan **Reduce, Recycle, and Reuse!**

Grade: Eight

Content objectives: science—solutions to environmental problems
(reduce, reuse, recycle), English language arts—writing for a purpose (to
influence)

Information skill objectives: Web site evaluation

Technology skill objectives: word processing, presentation software, such
as PowerPoint

Time estimate: Four extended class periods

> **?** **Information problem:** Now that we have studied environmental
> problems and the need to "reduce, reuse, and recycle," and
> understand the phrase "Think globally, act locally," how can we
> influence the student body to do its part around the school?

Big6 #1: Task Definition

#1.1 Present the problem to the class. Tell them that we will use the Big6
to help us solve the problem, starting with Task Definition. Put students
in groups of three to brainstorm a solution to this problem. List all
groups' ideas on the projector or board. Ask students to summarize the
ideas into one statement, such as, "Encourage all of the school
community to reduce, recycle, and reuse."

#1.2 Assign each group to research one of the methods of conserving
resources: reduce, recycle, or reuse. Several groups can have the same
concept. Instruct the groups to decide what information they will need to
know about their conservation method in order to convince others of its
importance and to practice the action. Ask the groups to write their list in
question form. After all are finished, go around to each group and discuss
their list, adding questions as needed. Tell students that they may uncover
more ideas in their research; they are not limited to these questions.

Reduce: What does it mean "to reduce?" How are companies trying to
reduce use of natural resources? What can students and teachers at the
school use less? How can the administration use fewer natural resources
around the school? How can we teach the school community to
"reduce?"

Recycle: What is recycling? How is the outside community recycling?
What materials can be recycled at school? How will the materials get to
the recycle center? What types of bins are needed? Where can these bins

be placed in the school? How can we teach the school community to "recycle?"

Reuse: What is reusing? How is the outside community reusing? What products can be reused at school? Are there paper products that instead of throwing away or recycling can be replaced with reusable ones? Which products can various departments of the school reuse? How can we teach the school community to reuse?

Big6 #2: Information Seeking Strategies

#2.1 Help groups brainstorm a list of sources in which they can find answers to their questions. Display and list all suggestions. Add human resources such as sanitation departments if students neglect to mention these.

#2.2 Choose the best sources for the class: library books, textbook, subscription databases, free Web sites, city water and sanitation departments, school principal, and maintenance personnel.

Show the Web Evaluation Guide that is used by the school. Choose one authoritative site about conservation and one that is of questionable accuracy and authority. Demonstrate to the class how to evaluate these for accuracy and authority (see Chapter Seven). Choose only two or three of the points in the Web Evaluation Guide for students to practice.

Big6 #3: Location and Access

#3.1 Review location of subscription databases and review advanced search in Google.

#3.2 Remind students to use the index in books. Review subject, keyword, and full-text searching. Groups that need to contact city employees should obtain phone numbers.

Big6 #4: Use of Information

#4.1 Students read appropriate sections in sources.

#4.2 Take notes on needed information using standard note taking form. Instruct students to cite sources. Groups can divide the questions for their conservation method to lessen the amount of note taking for each member of the group.

Big6 #5: Synthesis

#5.1 Group members organize notes and sketch their displays.

#5.2 Groups prepare an informational display to persuade students and teachers to reuse, recycle, or reduce. Each student writes the principal a letter persuading her to follow the conservation methods school-wide and encourage maintenance staff to do so. Students turn in notes, drafts, sketches, and Web evaluations. Present results orally to all social studies classes using the displays or PowerPoint slides as visuals.

Big6 #6: Evaluation

#6.1 Prepare scoring guide for each group to use as it researches, prepares its display or presentation, and as each student writes the letter to the principal.

#6.2 Each student responds to Group Evaluation (see Chapter Eleven).

Assessment: Scoring guide for Web evaluations, notes, display or presentation, group work, letter to principal.

Lesson Plan | You've Been Hired by BHO: Ancient Rome!

(Task Definition courtesy Mr. Bert Baetz, St. Andrew's Episcopal School, Austin, Texas)

Grade: Nine

Content objectives: Ancient history—Rome

Information skill objectives: Note taking—summarizing and paraphrasing, presentation skills

Technology skill objectives: Constructing effective PowerPoint slides to accompany oral presentation

> **?** **Information problem:** Pretend that you have been hired as consultants to BHO Pictures for their new miniseries titled *Ancient Rome*. Five teams will focus on a particular period in Rome's history, and each one of you will be assigned a specific job within your era. You will be an explorer, a political/military historian, or a cultural anthropologist. The producers from BHO Pictures formulated a number of questions in order to direct your research, and make sure you support your findings with accurate and authentic sources. The producers expect a quality presentation of your expert investigation!

Big6 #1: Task Definition

1.1 Teacher will assign each group of three or four to one of the time periods below. Tell students that they are not confined to researching just the questions presented, but are encouraged to find additional information that would enhance their content and their classmates' knowledge of the period and topic.

1.2 Due to students' lack of knowledge on the topic of Ancient Rome, the teacher will give them the following questions on which to research: (Questions for the Pinnacle of the Empire and the Decline and Fall of the Empire are not included in this lesson plan. Check <http://library.sasaustin.org/sasaustin/library/integratedAssignments/baetzRome/index.html> for additional questions.)

Group one: Origins and Age of the Republic (509–133 BC)

The role of the explorer:

William Duiker says, "Geography had an impact on Roman history" (121). Your job is to support his claim. What was the geography of "Rome" during your assigned time period? How far did Rome stretch during your time period? Who were Rome's neighbors? How did they interact or engage with their neighbors?

The role of the political and military historian:
How did the Romans engage in warfare during your time period? Did they have an army? A navy? Who is recruited to join the army? What implementations contribute to the success of Rome's military? You should refer to one specific battle in order to fill the military picture of Rome during this period. Also, describe the political structure of Rome during your assigned time period. How did it function? Who were the leader(s) or ruler(s)? What was a magistrate? Describe his role. How large was the senate? Does the size change?

The role of the cultural anthropologist:
What records do we have from this time period? Who wrote the records? What did the Romans record for their own purposes during your assigned time period? Identify and describe the architecture and other significant artifacts of this period. What inventions are attributed to Rome during this time period? Explain Rome's societal structure during your time period. How did it relate to the economy? Who were Roman citizens?

Group two: Decline and Fall of the Republic (133–31 BC)

The role of the explorer:
William Duiker says, "Geography had an impact on Roman history" (121). Your job is to support his claim. What was the geography of "Rome" during your assigned time period? How far did Rome stretch during your time period? Who were Rome's neighbors? How did they interact or engage with their neighbors?

The role of the political and military historian:
How did the Romans engage in warfare during your time period? Did they have an army? A navy? Describe the military system during your period. Refer to specific generals and battles. How does Rome recruit for the military? What implementations contribute to the success of Rome's military? You might refer to one specific battle in order to fill the military picture of Rome during this period. Also, describe the political structure of Rome during your time period. What led to the decline of a republican political structure? Who ruled during this time period? Where? What changes in rule occurred during this period? How did the Republic end?

The role of the cultural anthropologist:
Identify the literary/historical texts of this time period. Describe the architecture of this period. Explain Rome's societal structure during your time period. How did it relate to the economy? How did it

influence the government? What systems connect people to the great leaders of this age? What is life like in the provinces? What is it like to be a Roman citizen outside of Italy?

Group three: Rise of the Empire (27 BC–96 AD)

The role of the explorer:

William Duiker says, "Geography had an impact on Roman history" (121). Your job is to support his claim. What was the geography of "Rome" during your assigned time period? How far did Rome stretch during your time period? Who were Rome's neighbors? How did they interact or engage with their neighbors?

The role of the political and military historian:

Who was the first emperor of Rome? How did the transition occur? Who is the princeps? What is the significance of this title and position? What is the Prætorian Guard? What dynasty was established during this period? Describe the characteristics of the dynasty and its effects on the political structure.

The role of the cultural anthropologist:

What engineering accomplishments are attributed to this time period? What mathematical, scientific, and astronomical reforms and discoveries occurred during this time period? How were the emperors understood *religiously*? Describe the religion during this period. How does Rome react to the rise of Christianity? What monumental architecture was completed during this era?

Big6 #2: Information Seeking Strategies

Tell students that the best sources for their research are the following:

- Thomson Gale Student Resource Center
- EBSCOHost History Reference Center®
- Encyclopedia Britannica Online
- WebFeet™ links to academic Web sites on the free Web
- netTrekker® links to academic Web sites on the free Web
- In addition, the library has many books on reserve for this project.

Big6 #3: Location and Access

#3.1 Show students how to locate subscription databases from the school library's Web site.

#3.2 Instruct students in listing keywords and related words from their questions. Give these examples: geography—maps, regions; warfare—army, navy, military, military strategy; political structure—leaders, rulers, magistrate, senate; anthropology—artifacts, records, inventions, societal structure. They will use these words to search the databases and Web sites.

Big6 #4: Use of Information

#4.1 Use student-generated keywords and related words to look for essential points of access (see Chapter Nine).

#4.2 Instruct students that note taking will probably be:
A *combination of words and phrases* copied exactly from the source (to answer knowledge-level questions), *summarizing* (condensing large amounts of material into one or two sentences), and some *paraphrasing* (when they need to include most of the text of a published paragraph, but put into their own words instead of quoting or copying huge amounts of text). Review paraphrasing (see Chapter Nine).

Big6 #5: Synthesis

#5.1 Groups will organize their notes and plan for their oral presentations.

#5.2 Groups create PowerPoint slides adhering to the Visuals section of the Presentation Guidelines (see Part III). Each group will use PowerPoint to create an outline on which other members of the class will take notes. Demonstrate. Their oral presentation will adhere to the other sections in the Presentation Guidelines. The teacher will work closely with each group to make sure its findings are accurate and thoroughly presented for classmates.

Groups will print their slides (six to a page) to turn in with their notes and outline one day early so copies of the outline can be made for the class.

Groups present to the producers of BHO Pictures (their classmates), who will take notes on their presentations for a quiz on each era of Rome.

Big6 #6: Evaluation

Each group member fills out Group Evaluation (see Chapter Eleven) detailing his or her experiences with the project.

Assessment: Prepare scoring guides for notes and outlines, use Presentation Guidelines for assessing the slides and oral reports. Grade individual quizzes. These will be given several days after the presentations to give students enough time to study. Consider open-book quizzes.

Pathfinders

Guiding children to sources and providing strategies in accessing and using sources remains a critical responsibility of the library media specialist. Through collaboration with the subject-area teacher, the library media specialist can create pathfinders to guide students to the sources they will need for an assignment or big project. The pathfinder will serve as a reference for students after the library media specialist has instructed the class in accessing and using resources.

The library media specialist can use word processing or Web authoring software to construct pathfinders for students. The critical components will include, but are not limited to:

- Title of project or assignment
- List of sources available on the library shelves and in the classroom (textbook will be listed here if students use it as source)
- List of sources available online (both on the free Web as appropriate, and by subscription) with links to electronic materials
- Guide to accessing information within sources
- Instruction for how to use information within sources (note taking)
- Instructions on how to get help, if needed

Figure 12.6 is an example of a Roman History Project Pathfinder for ninth grade:

Additional points of instruction on the pathfinder may include details about the task, final product, and evaluation. Including all steps of the Big6 provides middle school students with "one-stop shopping," allowing them to concentrate more effort on the project instead of spending time piecing together its components (Figure 12.7). However, because pathfinders including all of the steps of the process may limit students need to interact with the process, use these prudently. In other words, as often as possible, give students opportunities to engage thoughtfully in each step of the Big6 by allowing them to construct each phase.

Figure 12.6: Roman History Project Pathfinder

Roman History Project Pathfinder
Big6™ Location and Access, Information

These reference sources will help you access materials for the Roman History Project. If you have questions about the resources, citing sources, or note taking, please contact *your librarian.* If you have questions about the assignment, please contact *your teacher.*

"Marcus Aurelius."
Image courtesy of The Gale Group

"The ancient ruins of the Coliseum in Rome."
Image courtesy of The Gale Group

Books on reserve in the School Library

History:
Latin literatures: a history 870.9 CON
Great books 909 DEN
Cambridge ancient history 937 CAM
Daily life in ancient Rome 937 CAR
Gibbon I and II 937 GIB
History of Rome under the emperors 937 MOM
History of the Roman people 937 WAR
The Greek achievement 938 FRE

Reference:
Greek and Latin authors 800BC - AD1000 REF 880 GRA
Oxford companion to classical literature REF 880.9 HOW
World eras; Roman republic and empire v.3 REF 904 WOR
World eras: Classical Greek civilization v.6 REF904 WOR
Literature and its times v.1 REF 809 MOS
Ancient Europe 8000BC - AD1000 REF 936 ANC
The ancient and medieval world REF 930 HIS
Oxford classical dictionary REF 938 OXF

Resources from school's subscription databases

All of these reference databases are available on our *Subscription database page*

Gale Group: Student Resource Center Gold

EBSCO Student Research Center

Proquest: eLibrary

Encyclopaedia Britannica Middle School Edition

Don't neglect to look at the related links and various other links that come up for each search. See your librarian for passwords if you are using the databases at home.

Sites on the free Web: (You don't need to evaluate these Web sites. However, if you use any not listed here, or if you click on links that take you out of these sites, you will need to complete a Web site evaluation for each that you use.[Web site evaluation guide]
http://www.forumromanum.org/history/index.html
http://www.roman-empire.net/

Take notes on the form that is provided and cite your sources on the form. You need to use a new form every time you change sources or topics. [Note taking form] [Help with citing sources]

Figure 12.7: Body Systems Pathfinder

Big6™ Pathfinder
Disorders of Human Body Systems

Big6 #1:Task Definition

Now that we have studied all of the human body systems and know their functions, what can we do to keep them healthy? What disorders and diseases can strike, and do we have any control over them?

1.1 You will be assigned one organ system. Learn about how to keep it healthy and what diseases and disorders may affect it. The organ systems we will study are: integumentary, muscular, skeletal, cardio-vascular, respiratory, urinary, reproductive (male and female), nervous, lymphatic, digestive, and endocrine.

2.2 Brainstorm what you need to find out about your organ system. After your group develops a list of questions that you need to research, Mrs. Lewis will provide additional questions that you need to consider.

Big6 #2: Information Seeking Strategies; Big6 #3: Location & Access

Books on reserve in the School Library
List books here

Subscription databases: All of these reference databases are available on our *Subscription database page*

Gale Group: Student Resource Center Gold and Health Module

EBSCO Student Research Center

Proquest; eLibrary

Encyclopaedia Britannica Middle School Edition

Don't neglect to look at the related links and various other links that come up for each search. See your librarian for passwords if you need to use the databases at home.

Sites on the free Web: (You don't need to evaluate these Web sites.) You may not use any other Web sites unless you get them approved by your librarian or teacher.

http://www.ahealthwebsite.org; www.anotherhealthsite.com; www.yetanotherwebsiteabouthealth.net

Big6 #4: Use of Information

Take notes on the form that is provided and cite your sources on the form. You need to use a new form every time you change sources or topics.
Note taking form
Help with citing sources

Big6 #5: Synthesis

5.1 Combine your notes with those of your partners'. Look again at the questions you are required to answer. Do you need more notes, have enough, or need to discard some information?

5.2 Part One: Design a pamphlet (tri-fold) that may be found in a health clinic that discusses ways someone can take care of the body system you researched. Include diseases and disorders that the person may need to be aware of and whether or not these are genetic or can be prevented, including ways to prevent them.

Part Two: Make a presentation that a doctor may use to talk to a patient about that body system's healthcare, diseases, and disorders. Present to your classmates. Mrs. Lewis will need to approve your presentation method before you start. Include a bibliography of sources you consulted.

Big6 #6: Evaluation

____what I created to finish the assignment is what I was supposed to do in Big6 #5.2

____most of the information I found in Big6 #4 matches the information needed in Big6 #1

____credit is given to my sources, written in standard citation format

____my work is neat

____my work is complete and includes heading information (name, date)

____I would be proud for anyone to view this work

Part III: Big6 Cool Tools

Barbara A. Jansen

Big6 Assignment Organizer for Grades 5-6

Name: _____   Period:___   Date: _____

★★ Fill out Big6 #1-5 *before* you begin to work on your assignment.
★★ Fill out Big6 #6 *before* you turn in your assignment.

Big6 #1: Task Definition

What am I supposed to do?

What information do I need in order to do this? (List these in question form.)

1.
2.
3.
4.
5.
6.
7.
8.
9.
10.
11.
12.

Big6 #2 Information Seeking Strategies

What sources can I use to find this information?	If using Web sites, how will I know that they are good enough for my project?
1. 2. 3. 4. 5.	___ I will use only those given to me by my teachers and librarian. ___ I will ask my librarian, teacher, or parent for help in finding good Web sites for my project.

Big6 #3: Location and Access

Where will I find these sources?	Who can help me find what I need?
____school library ____public library ____my own library at home ____provided by my teachers ____Internet ____Other: _____ _____	____my librarian ____my teacher ____my parents ____I can find the sources myself

Big6 #4: Use of Information

How will I record the information that I find?	How will I give credit to my sources?
___ take notes using cards ___ take notes on notebook paper ___ take notes using a word processor ___ take notes using a data chart ___ Illustrate concepts ___ talk into a tape recorder ___ other_____	___use the guide given to me by my teacher ___use a Web site that creates citations ___write citations by hand ___other_____

Big6 #5: Synthesis

How will I show my results?	How will I give credit to my sources in my final product or performance?
___ written paper ___ multimedia project _____ _____ ___ performance or presentation _____ _____ ___ other_____	___include a written bibliography ___after the performance, announce which sources I used ___write citations by hand ___other_____

Big6 #6: Evaluation

How will I know if I have done my best? Before turning in the assignment, I need to check off all of these items:

___ what I created to finish the assignment is what I was supposed to do in Big6 #1
___ most of the information I found in Big6 #4 matches the information needed in Big6 #1
___ credit is given to my sources, written in the way my teacher assigned
___ my work is neat
___ my work is complete and includes heading information (name, date)
___ I would be proud for anyone to view this work

Include here any additional information needed to successfully complete assignment:

Date due: _____

Notes due: _____

First draft due: _____

Materials needed:

Group members:

Big6' Assignment Organizer for Grades 7-9

The BIG 6

Name: _____ **Period:___ Date:** _____

★★ Fill out Big6 #1-5 *before* you begin to work on your assignment.
★★ Fill out Big6 #6 *before* you turn in your assignment.

Big6 #1: Task Definition

What am I supposed to do?

What information do I need in order to do this? (Use space on back if more is needed.)

1.
2.
3.
4.
5.
6.
7.
8.
9.
10.
11.
12.

Big6 #2 Information Seeking Strategies

List the best sources to find this information.	If using Web sites, who will evaluate them for relevancy, accuracy and authority?
1. 2. 3. 4. 5.	___ I will use only those evaluated by and provided by my teachers. ___ I will use a Web site evaluation checklist provided by my teacher or library media specialist.

Big6 #3: Location and Access

Where will I find these sources?	Who can help me find what I need?
____school library ____public library ____my own library at home ____provided by my teachers ____Internet ____other: _____ _____	____my librarian ____my teacher ____my parents ____I can find the sources myself

Big6 #4: Use of Information

How will I record the information that I find?	How will I give credit to my sources?
___ take notes using cards	___use MLA or APA style
___ take notes on notebook paper	___use a Web site that creates citations
___ take notes using a word processor	___write citations by hand
___ take notes using a data chart	___use footnotes
___ illustrate concepts	
___ talk into a tape recorder	
___ other_____	

Big6 #5: Synthesis

What product or performance will I make to finish the assignment?	How will I give credit to my sources in my final product or performance?
___ written paper	___include a written bibliography
___ multimedia project	___after the performance, announce which sources I used
_____	___other_____
_____	
___ performance or presentation	
_____	
_____	
___ other_____	

Big6 #6: Evaluation

Before turning in the assignment, I need to check off all of these items:

___ what I created to finish the assignment is what I was supposed to do in Big6 #1

___ most of the information I found in Big6 #4 matches the information needed in Big6 #1

___ credit is given to my sources, written in standard citation format

___ my work is neat

___ my work is complete and includes heading information (name, date)

___ I would be proud for anyone to view this work

Include here any additional information needed to successfully complete assignment:

Date due: _____

Notes due: _____

First draft due: _____

Materials needed:

Group members:

The Big6 Writing Process Organizer for Grades 5-6

Big6 #1: Task Definition—What do I need to do?

This is the beginning of the first step of the writing process: *Prewriting*

1. What does your teacher want you to do? Ask your teacher to explain if you don't understand.

Write what it is you are supposed to do (in your own words):

2. What information do you need to include in your writing assignment? Ask your teacher if you don't know. Write a list of questions here so you will know what information to "look up" for your paper:

   1.
   2.
   3.
   4.
   5.
   6.
   7.
   8.

3. Put a check mark by any question above in which you will need to find answers in sources such as books, people, and Web sites.

Big6 #2: Information Seeking Strategies— What can I use to find what I need?

1. You need to make a list of all the possible sources of information (such as books and Web sites) that will help you answer the questions you checked in Big6 #1 Task Definition above. Ask your teacher, your librarian, or another adult to help you.

Make a list here:

2. Now, place a check mark beside each item to which you have access and are able to use. Ask your librarian for help if needed.

Big6 #3: Location & Access—Where can I find what I need?

1. Figure out where you will get these sources. Beside each source above, write its location. If it is a Web site, list its web address. Try to use those Web sites to which your school subscribes. Ask your librarian about these. This will save you time. If your source is a person, figure out how you will contact him or her and make a note of this.

2. Now, you will actually get the sources. You may have to get and use them one at a time. If so, come back to this step to locate each source.

3. Once you have the source in hand, you must get to the information within the source. Ask your librarian, teacher, or parent for help if needed.

Big6 #4: Use of Information—What information can I use?

1. Read, view, or listen to the sources you have located above. Take notes to answer the questions you wrote in Big6 #1.

2. Take notes on some kind of paper or card. Write just the words that answer your questions.

3. You must give credit to your sources. Ask for help if needed.

Big6 #5: Synthesis—How can I put my information together?

Now it is time to complete the writing process. You should talk to your teacher or librarian if you need help with this.

1. *Prewriting:* You have already completed the note taking part of this step. Now you need to brainstorm (make a list of) original ideas you will include in your paper. Write your ideas on note cards or notebook paper.

2. *Drafting:* Write the first version of your paper. Be sure to include the notes you took from your sources. Make sure you give credit to the books, people, and Web sites you used.

3. *Conferencing:* Ask your teacher to talk to you about your paper. Be prepared with at least two questions you would like answered about your paper.

4. *Revising:* During this part of the process, look at and think about what you have written. Your paper should be more than other people's ideas or what you found in Web sites. It should include at lot of your original ideas as well. Make sure it is what your teacher wants you to do for the paper. Make changes to make it better.

   You may want to combine short sentences and begin to look at your use of grammar. Revision makes good writing even better.

   You may need to talk to your teacher again after you revise your paper. Again, have one or two questions ready to ask about your paper.

5. *Editing:* This may be the most important part of the process. Your teacher or other trusted adult should give you ideas about improving your grammar and spelling, if needed. You must correct all errors.

6. *Publishing:* Try to use a word processor to write your final paper. If you don't have a computer, print or write neatly. Make sure you include a list of the books, people, and Web sites you used. This is called a bibliography. The bibliography should be alphabetized by author. Ask your teacher or librarian if you do not know how to write a bibliography.

Does your teacher also want you to make a product to go with your paper? Now is the time to make it.

Even though there are several steps to the writing process, it is very important for you to talk to an adult at each step and understand that you can go back to and repeat any step at any time during the process.

Big6 #6: Evaluation—How will I know if I did well?

Before you show your paper (and product) to others, be sure it is as perfect as you can make it. This paper should be something you are proud to put your name on.
   Answer "yes" to all of these questions **before** you turn in your paper:

1. Did you do everything and include all that was required for the paper?

2. Does your final paper show your original ideas as well as other information you found?

3. Did you give credit to all of your sources, including a written bibliography?

4. Is your paper word processed (or very neatly typed or handwritten if you do not have access to a computer)?

5. Is your paper complete and does it include a title page with heading information (title, your name, your teacher's name, date)?

6. If your teacher asks for these, did you include your notes and copies of each version and your list of books, people, and Web sites?

7. Would you be proud for anyone to read this paper?

8. Do you understand each step of the Big6 and writing processes? If not, who can you ask for help?

Works consulted:

Carroll, Joyce Armstrong and Edward E. Wilson. *Acts of Teaching: How to Teach Writing.* Englewood, CO: Teacher Idea Press, 1993.

McGhee, Maria W. Assistant Professor. Educational Administration & Psychological Services Southwest Texas State University, San Marcos, Texas. Telephone interview. November 7, 2002.

The Big6 Writing Process Organizer for Grades 7-9

Big6 #1: Task Definition

1. Prewriting is the first step of the writing process. What does your teacher want you to do? Make sure you understand the requirements of the writing assignment. Ask your teacher to explain the assignment if it seems vague or confusing. Restate the assignment to your teacher in your own words and ask if you are correct. Write the assignment here in your own words:

2. What information do you need to include in your writing assignment? Write a list of questions to which you need to "find answers."

  *

  *

  *

  *

  *

3. Put a check mark beside any questions on the list that require you to find information in an outside source such as a library book or an online database.

Big6#2: Information Seeking Strategies

1. List all of the possible sources of information that will help you answer the questions you checked in Big6 #1 Task Definition. Consider library books, encyclopedias, and Web sites to which your library subscribes (ask your librarian!), people who are experts in your subject, observation of your subject, free Web sites, and surveys.

Make a list here:

*

*

*

*

*

2. Put a check mark beside each item to which you have access and are able to use. If you need help, ask your librarian.

Big6 #3: Location & Access

1. Figure out where you will find these sources. Write the location of each source beside each item on the list in Big6 #2 Information Seeking Strategies. If it is a Web site, list the Web address. Try to use those online databases to which your school subscribes. Ask your librarian about these to save time. If your source is a person, figure out how you will contact him or her and make a note of this.

2. Find the sources. You may need to get and use some sources one at a time. If so, come back to this step after you locate and use each source.

3. Once you have the source in hand, you must find the information within the source. If you need help, ask your librarian, teacher, or parent.

Big6 #4: Use of Information

1. Read, view, or listen to the sources you located during Big6 #3 Location & Access. Take notes to answer the questions you wrote in Big6 #1 Task Definition.

2. Take notes on note cards, a data chart, a word processing document, or notebook paper. Try to paraphrase or summarize ideas instead of just copying information word-for-word from your sources. Be sure to cite (give credit to) your sources.

Big6 #5: Synthesis

Now it is time to complete the writing process. You should talk to your teacher or librarian if you need help with this.

1. *Prewriting:* You have already completed the note taking part of this step. Brainstorm other ideas you will include in your paper. Write your ideas on note cards,

a data chart, a word processing document, or notebook paper. (You may want to use the same type of organizer that you used for your note taking in Big6 #4 Use of Information.)

2. *Drafting:* Write the first draft of your paper. Include the notes you took from your sources. Give credit to all the appropriate sources.

3. *Conferencing:* Ask your teacher for a content conference. Prepare at least two questions you would like answered about your paper. Focus on the content of your work rather than the grammar and spelling at this step.

4. *Revising:* During this part of the process, you will re-enter your writing. This is an opportunity for you to "re see" (reVISION) your writing in a different way. Your paper should be more than just a summary of other people's ideas or what you found on the Internet. It should represent mostly your ideas and conclusions. It should be a thoughtful response to the assignment. Make changes to improve your work.

   You may want to combine short sentences and begin to look at your use of grammar. Revising makes good writing even better.

   Think about scheduling another content conference with your teacher after you revise your paper. Again, have one or two questions ready to ask about your paper.

5. *Editing:* This may be the most important part of the writing process. Your teacher or other trusted adult should give you ideas about ways to improve your grammar and spelling, if needed. You need to correct all errors. You may choose to have a peer edit your paper. Choose someone who is a good writer!

6. *Publishing:* Use a word processor to publish your final paper. Include footnotes or parenthetical references, a bibliography, and any other parts of the paper as assigned. The bibliography should be arranged in alphabetical order by author's last name. Ask your teacher or librarian for information about how to write a bibliography.

   Does your assignment include a product to go with your paper? If so, now is the time to make the product.

   **Even though there are several steps to the writing process, it is very important to ask for feedback. You may repeat any step at any time during the process.*

Big6 #6: Evaluation

Before you show your paper (and product) to an audience, be sure it is as perfect as you can make it. You should be proud to put your name on your paper.

You should be able to answer "yes" to these questions before you turn in your paper:

1. Is your final paper a thoughtful response to the assignment?
2. Does your final paper represent your ideas and conclusions?
3. Is your paper more than just a summary of other people's ideas?
4. If you paraphrased or summarized information found in books or magazines, on the Internet, or from other people, did you cite the source at point of use in your paper (using a footnote or parenthetical reference)?
5. Did you give credit to all of your sources in a bibliography?
6. Did you do everything in the assignment?
7. Does your bibliography follow the MLA format? Find out if your teacher requires a format other than MLA.
8. Is your paper word processed (or very neatly typed or hand-written if you do not have access to a computer)?
9. Is your paper complete and does it include a title page with heading information (title, your name, your teacher's name, date)?
10. If your teacher requests these, did you include your notes, copies of each draft, and an annotated bibliography?
11. Would you be proud for anyone to read this paper?
12. Do you understand each step of the Big6 and writing processes? If not, who can you ask for help?

Bibliography:

1. Carroll, Joyce Armstrong and Edward E. Wilson. *Acts of Teaching: How to Teach Writing.* Englewood, CO: Teacher Idea Press, 1993.

2. McGhee, Marla W. Assistant Professor. Educational Administration & Psychological Services. Southwest Texas State University, San Marcos, Texas. Telephone interview. November 7, 2002.

The Big6 History Fair Process Organizer

Big6 #1: Task Definition—What do I need to do?

1. Choose a topic based on the current theme for the History Fair. Ask your teacher or another adult to help, use the Idea Generator at the end of this document.

   What is your topic?

2. What information do you need to research about your topic? Ask your teacher if you don't know. Write a list of questions here so you will know what information to "look up" for your paper. Use the back of this sheet if you run out of room.

   1.

   2.

   3.

   4.

   5.

   6.

   7.

   8.

3. Put a check mark by any question above in which you will need to find answers in sources such as books, people, and Web sites.

4. Choose a format in which you will display the results of your work: build an exhibit, write a historical paper, produce an audio visual documentary, or create a dramatic performance. You will create your product in Big6 #5: Synthesis.

Big6 #2: Information Seeking Strategies—What can I use to find what I need?

1. You need to make a list of all the possible sources of information (such as books and Web sites) that will help you answer the questions you checked in Big6 #1 Task Definition above. Ask your teacher, your librarian, or another adult to help you.

Make a list here:

2. Now, place a check mark beside each item to which you have access and are able to use. Ask your librarian for help if needed.

Big6 #3: Location & Access—Where can I find what I need?

1. Figure out where you will get these sources. Beside each source above, write its location. If it is a Web site, list its Web address. Try to use those Web sites to which your school subscribes. Ask your librarian about these. This will save you time. If your source is a person, figure out how you will contact him or her and make a note of this.

2. Now, you will actually get the sources. You may have to get and use them one at a time. If so, come back to this step to locate each source.

3. Once you have the source in hand, you must get to the information within the source. Ask your librarian, teacher, or parent for help if needed.

Big6 #4: Use of Information—What information can I use?

1. Read, view, or listen to the sources you have located above. Take notes to answer the questions you wrote in Big6 #1.

2. Take notes on some kind of note taking organizer or card. Write just the words that answer your questions. Ask your teacher or librarian for help if you don't know how to take notes.

3. You must give credit to your sources. Ask for help if needed.

Big6 #5: Synthesis—How can I put my information together?

Now it is time to complete your project. You should talk to your teacher or librarian if you need help. Make sure that you follow all official guidelines for the History Fair. If not, you may be disqualified. Ask your teacher for these guidelines.

If you are writing a historical paper, you may use the steps of the writing process below to ensure a quality effort:

1. *Prewriting:* You have already completed the note taking part of this step. Now you need to brainstorm (make a list of) original ideas you will include in your paper. Write your ideas on note cards or notebook paper.

2. *Drafting:* Write the first version of your paper. Be sure to include the notes you took from your sources. Make sure you give credit to the books, people, and Web sites you used.

3. *Conferencing:* Ask your teacher to talk to you about your paper. Be prepared with at least two questions you would like answered about your paper.

4. *Revising:* During this part of the process, look at and think about what you have written. Your paper should be more than other people's ideas or what you found in Web sites. It should include a lot of your original ideas as well. Make sure it is what your teacher wants you to do for the paper. Make changes to make it better.

   You may want to combine short sentences and begin to look at your use of grammar. Revision makes good writing even better.

   You may need to talk to your teacher again after you revise your paper. Again, have one or two questions ready to ask about your paper.

5. *Editing:* This may be the most important part of the process. Your teacher or other trusted adult should give you ideas about improving your grammar and spelling, if needed. You must correct all errors.

6. *Publishing:* Try to use a word processor to write your final paper. If you don't have a computer, print or write neatly. Make sure you include a list of the books, people, and Web sites you used. This is called a bibliography. The bibliography should be alphabetized by author. Ask your teacher or librarian if you do not know how to write a bibliography.

   ***Even though there are several steps to the writing process, it is very important for you to talk to an adult at each step and understand that you can go back to and repeat any step at any time during the process.*

Big6 #6: Evaluation—How will I know if I did well?

 Before you take your project to school or to the History Fair site, be sure it is as perfect as you can make it. This product should be something you are proud to put your name on.

Answer "yes" to all of these questions **before** you turn in your product:

1. Did you do everything and include all that was required for the product?
2. Does your final product show your original ideas as well as other information you found?
3. Did you follow all official guidelines for the History Fair? This is very important!
4. Did you give credit to all of your sources, including a written bibliography?
5. Would you be proud for anyone to see or read your project?
8. Do you understand each step of the Big6? If not, who can you ask for help?

Works consulted:

Carroll, Joyce Armstrong and Edward E. Wilson. *Acts of Teaching: How to Teach Writing.* Englewood, CO: Teacher Idea Press, 1993.

McGhee, Marla W. Assistant Professor. Educational Administration & Psychological Services. Southwest Texas State University, San Marcos, Texas. Telephone interview. November 7, 2002.

Big6™ Science Fair Project Organizer

Name: _____ **Date:** _____

Big6 #1 Task Definition

1. **Choose a topic for study.** Here is a way to start: Observe the world around you. What interests you about it? What hobbies do you like to do? If you cannot think of anything, ask your teacher for the Idea Generator available in *Teaching Information and Communications Technology Skills: The Big6™ in Middle Schools*. Make a list of topics here:

a. Look at the topics on your list. How can you turn one of those interests into a scientific study (a question to explore) that you will enjoy and will capture the interest of those who view it?

b. Write your topic here:

2. **Make your topic into a question that you will answer by conducting an experiment.**

Write your question here:

3. **Make a hypothesis**—predict what you think the answer to your question might be. You can rephrase the question into a statement.

Write the hypothesis here:

4. **Begin your background research**. First make a list of questions that you need to find out about your topic before you start.

   Make a list of questions here:

   You will actually do the reading and note taking in Use of Information (Big6 #4) below.

5. **Develop a method**. You need to figure out a way to prove or disprove (test) your hypothesis. This is the experiment you will perform on your subject. The outcome should be measurable. This means that you should be able to tell how much or how little (usually in numbers) your hypothesis was proven or disproven. Your method should be observation and experimentation. Consider the amount of time you need for the study and when the project is due. For example: Plant growth experiments take weeks to complete. Plan carefully!

   Describe your method here (talk to your teacher or parent if you need help):

How much time will you need for this project? Consider that scientists repeat their experiments several times in order to confirm their results. Try to plan time to do the experiment at least two times. Ask your science teacher how many repeats or sets of the experiment you should do.

When is it due? If parts are due separately, then create a calendar or timeline.

Do you have time to do this study? If not, start over at number 1.

Big6 #2 Information Seeking Strategies

1. You will need **sources** for background information. Brainstorm a list of these sources in which you can find background information for your topic. Consider using library books, scientific magazines, experts on your topic, and databases to which your library subcribes. Use free Web sites if you can't find anything else. Ask your librarian for help!

Make a list here:

Now decide which will be the best to use because you can find them (or have someone help you find them). Circle them in the list above.

2. **Materials** you think you will need for your experiment.

Make a list here:

Who can help you get these materials?

Big6 #3 Location & Access

1. **Locate** the sources for your background information. Your librarian can help you find the books and Web sites you need.
2. **Gather** the materials you will need for your experiment (the materials you listed in #1 above).

You will probably need your teacher's or your parent's help getting the materials. Include a notebook in your materials so you can record all of your experimentation method, observations, and data.

Big6 #4 Use of Information

1. **Answer** the questions you developed for your background information (Big6 #1 Task Definition number 4 above) by reading and taking notes. Write down anything else that is interesting about your topic of study. Be sure to cite your sources (this means to give credit to the sources because you borrowed from them).

2. **Conduct the experiment** you designed in the Method section above (Big6 #1 Task Definition number 5). Take notes and keep careful records on everything you do. Take photographs of each step of the experiment to use when you display the results. This may take several days or weeks. Record your results. Scientists repeat the experiment in order to confirm their results. Do this the number of times you planned in the method section in Task Definition above).

Big6 #5 Synthesis

1. **Draw a conclusion.** State whether your hypothesis was proven or not and explain the results.
2. **Make a plan to display** your question, hypothesis, method, conclusion, and the results. Your background information and data can be displayed in a notebook or report. You can include the written process in the report also. Using charts and graphs, help your audience understand your data. Don't forget to include a bibliography (list of sources you used for your background information).

3. **Make a list of what you will need for the display**. A tri-fold poster board (to set behind your materials) is available at many hobby shops or office supply stores.

4. **Create the display**. Be sure to include a title and your name on the tri-fold poster. Use a word processor instead of handwriting the

display and report. Include graphics and pictures (possibly photographs) to help your audience understand what you were trying to do. Include a shortened version of the process on your display. Here is where you will use your photos to help the judges and audience understand what was included in the steps of the study. Include some of your materials and show as much of the experiment as you can.

5. **Present your findings**. Be ready to talk to the judges about your process and results and answer questions from people visiting your project.

Big6 #6 Evaluation

Before you take your project to school or to the science fair, answer the following questions to make sure that you have done your best work:

1. **Evaluate** your method.

Was the method the best way to prove or disprove the hypothesis? If you answered no, then what would you change about the method? Add this to your conclusion.

2. **Evaluate** your background research.

Did your background research give you adequate information about your subject to get you started on planning your experiment? If not, what information should you have researched? Is it too late to add this information to your report?

3. **Evaluate** your display.

- Does your display contain your name and a title?
- Is it word processed, neat, and organized using headings and subheadings?
- Do the text, graphics, and photographs extend the judges' and audience's understanding of your process and results?
- Are your materials safe? Can your materials break or spill and harm young children who may look at your project? If so, how can you make the materials safe? This is very important!
- Would you be proud for anyone to view this project?

Presentation Guidelines for Middle School

The BIG 6

Name: _____ **Date:** _____

The ability to present yourself in a professional and effective manner is a skill you will use for a lifetime. The following guidelines are just that—guidelines. They are by no means an absolute or comprehensive directive for the content and style of your presentations. Keep in mind that presenting to an audience is difficult. Rehearse several times. Don't worry if you don't do everything perfectly the first time. Try your best, and keep looking back at these guidelines. Always ask yourself, "Is this information getting across effectively to a classmate who is hearing it for the first time?"

Your successful presentation has four components in which you must consider: content, organization, speaking and presenting skills, and visuals. If you are presenting with a group of your classmates, there are criteria for groups also. Read these guidelines before you begin, and again when you are finished planning your presentation, so you can make corrections well in advance of your presentation.

Content

Consider that you are not just showing what you learned, but that you are contributing to your classmates' knowledge and helping them learn the material you researched. Develop your content with this in mind.

The following points should be considered when developing your content:

☐ Research thoroughly so that you have a rich understanding of your subject matter, with the ability to answer questions from your audience.

☐ Ensure that the majority of your content and many of your ideas are original and inventive and based upon logical conclusions and thorough research.

☐ Include complete and accurate information.

☐ Engage your audience with rich content, enthusiasm, and eagerness to encourage them to want to learn more.

☐ Devise ways to help your classmates understand and relate to the content, such as giving examples or relating concepts to something they know or have already studied.

☐ Explain or define difficult concepts and vocabulary.

☐ Include meaningful audience involvement or participation, if that will help them understand the content.

☐ Use visuals to support or extend the content.

☐ Properly cite sources according to MLA style or one your teacher specifies. Do this orally or on a visual.

Organization

The organization of your presentation shows evidence of your preparation and attention to detail. If your presentation is organized and polished, your classmates will be able to focus on your content and message.

Consider the following criteria when organizing your presentation:

☐ Include a greeting and an introduction of yourself and your topic.

☐ Use an introduction that engages the audience and is related to the content—a "hook" to get the audience interested.

☐ Follow a logical sequence.

☐ Maintain a fluent pace. (This takes practice!)

☐ If you are using PowerPoint slides as prompts, elaborate on brief points instead of reading lengthy text off each slide.

☐ Involve your audience in a meaningful way, allowing time for them to think and respond.

☐ Logically conclude the presentation.

☐ Rehearse several times.

Speaking and Presenting Skills

How you present yourself to your audience makes or breaks your presentation. Practice many times so that you are confident and can concentrate on the content and your audience during the presentation.

Keep the following points in mind as you prepare and present your presentation:

☐ Show confidence. (Preparation and practice will help this!)

☐ Know your content well enough so you don't need to be prompted or to read extensively from notes.

☐ Show enthusiasm for your topic.

☐ Use an interested, conversational tone of voice.

☐ Use humor, as appropriate, to connect to or extend the content. Refrain from silliness and inappropriate laughter.

☐ Make eye contact with various members of the audience.

☐ Use good posture and dress appropriately.

- [ ] Use body movement for effect only, otherwise stand still when speaking.
- [ ] Stay within two minutes of allotted time.
- [ ] Refrain from using empty words and fillers, such as "uh, like, you know, uhm."
- [ ] Remove chewing gum before presenting.

Visuals and PowerPoint

Visuals should support or extend the oral component of your presentation. They must be well-constructed and easy for your audience to see.

Some ideas for visuals include:

- PowerPoint slide show (see below for PowerPoint guidelines)
- Poster
- Photograph
- Model
- Transparency
- Video
- Real object
- Map
- Illustration
- Hand-out (attractive, well-organized with relevant information)
- Outline of your presentation to help your classmates take notes

PowerPoint Slide Show Guidelines

Before you create a PowerPoint slide show, ask yourself this question: "Is this the best format to aid in presenting the results of my research findings and conclusions?" If you answer "yes," consider the following criteria when creating your slide show:

- [ ] Begin with an introductory slide including your topic and the names of the presenters.
- [ ] Each slide should contain main points, not the entire text of your presentation. You should use the points for elaboration. Give your classmates a reason to have to listen to you and take notes if needed.
- [ ] Font size should be no smaller than 32 points and the style should be consistent throughout the slide show.
- [ ] Font color should contrast with the background color. Font color, typeface, and contrast should be visible. You should not have to turn off the lights to read your slides.

- [ ] Text animation should be used sparingly, if at all. Use it to make a point, not to entertain. Overuse of animation will distract your audience.
- [ ] Images should reinforce or extend the content and be visible from the back of the room. Be careful—text may be difficult to read if superimposed over graphics.
- [ ] Use a lot of "white space," refraining from cluttering each slide.
- [ ] Use sound prudently—only for extending or supporting the content.
- [ ] Slide transitions should be consistent throughout the presentation.
- [ ] If linking to Web sites, those should also be visible from the back of the room.
- [ ] Use correct grammar, spelling, punctuation, and capitalization.
- [ ] Include a "Works Cited" slide, giving credit to the sources of information you used.
- [ ] Include an opening slide stating that your project contains copyrighted materials (if indeed it does), which have been used under the fair use exemption of the U.S. Copyright Law. If you have made alterations, those must be indicated.
- [ ] Try to rehearse your presentation with the computer connected to the projection device.

Group Presentations

Many careers require you to problem-solve with other colleagues, presenting results to a boss, board of directors, or a committee. Working in a group should be a good experience, but can also be stressful if you don't share the work load and cooperate.

The following points can help ease the stress and produce a polished presentation:

- [ ] Follow the guidelines in the other sections: Content, Organization, Visuals, Speaking, and Presenting Skills.
- [ ] Share the work load.
- [ ] Contribute the same effort you would to an individual assignment.
- [ ] Include complete and accurate information.
- [ ] Make the presentation look unified—not like separate presentations put together.
- [ ] Give equal presentation time to each group member.
- [ ] Practice together several times before the actual presentation.

Instructional Unit Planning Guide

Unit or curriculum standard:

Information Problem—How can the unit (or specific curriculum standard) be presented as an authentic and motivating information problem for students to engage? The problem should cause students to *need* to and *want* to engage in the content.

Big6 #1.1—What is the students' task? (Learn about...)

How can the students help define the task without you initially telling them? (You may have to modify the task as defined by the students so that the curriculum standards are covered.)

Big6 #1.2—What information do the students need to know in order to accomplish the task? (List these in question form.) Use the other side if necessary.

Big6 #2.1 and #2.2—Which sources are students most likely to use for this unit? Consider having students use library books and the online and CD-ROM databases to which the library subscribes before using sources off the free Web. (Consider human resources such as interviews, survey, and observation whenever appropriate.)

How will students obtain a list of sources?

☐ brainstorm (with or without assistance) to create comprehensive list
☐ other

Which additional sources will you introduce to the students?

Big6 #3.1—Where will students locate these sources?

What instruction do students need in specific location skills? (Consider online or card catalog, keyword searching, shelf arrangement, Boolean operators (and, or, not), telephone book use, Internet search engines)

Big6 #3.2—What instruction do students need in accessing information within the source? (Consider index and table of contents, keyword identification and listing related words, various search options on subscription databases)

Big6 #4.1—How will students engage in the source? (Read, listen, view, touch)

Other considerations about the contents of the sources (reliability, bias, currency, etc. especially when using Web sites)—can be completed in Big6 #2

Who will evaluate Web sites for authority and accuracy and judge for relevancy?

☐ teacher or librarian

☐ students (consider having student complete a formal Web evaluation for each free site used)

Big6 #4.2—How will students take from the source the information they need (note taking)?

___ trash and treasure method of note taking for factual information

___ summarizing and paraphrasing for older students, as developmentally appropriate

On which type of organizer will students use to record notes?

___ data chart
___ note cards
___ electronic organizer (MS Word, Inspiration)
___ other (such as Venn diagram, comparison chart, cluster diagram)

What instruction will students need prior to taking notes?

Big6 #5.1—How will students organize the information from all of their sources?

___ written rough draft   ___ graphic organizer
___ sketch   ___ other
___ roughly drawn plan

Consider: How, by going beyond the given information, will students add value to the knowledge-level information found in sources?

Big6 #5.2—How will students display their results?

___ product   ___ presentation
___ paper   ___ other

What higher-level thinking and transferable skills are included in the final product?

How can students show results in a written format, such as an essay or other paper?

What materials and instruction will students need?

Will students choose their own product (with or without guidance)?

How will students give credit to their sources?
___ bibliography
___ spoken credit during a presentation

Big6 #6.1 and #6.2—How will students evaluate their own efforts?

___ predetermined set of criteria such as a rubric or scoring guide
___ informal written evaluation
___ both
___ other

Who will create the rubric or scoring guide?
___ teacher and librarian
___ student input in descriptors
___ other

Additional Considerations

What are the content objectives?

What are the specific information problem-solving (Big6) objectives on which you will focus?

What prerequisite skills or content objectives do students need before beginning this sequence of instruction?

What audience will the students have for their efforts?

How will the teacher and librarian be involved with the class or individuals while the other is teaching?

How are the students going to be grouped?
___ individual
___ group of three or four
___ pair
___ other

What materials are needed and who is responsible for collecting them?

What is the time frame?

How will the unit be evaluated by the teacher or librarian?

How will you celebrate and advertise the students' products or performances and information searching accomplishments?

Big6 Skills copyright 1990, Eisenberg and Berkowitz. Instructional Unit Planning Guide copyright 2003, Barbara A. Jansen.

Evaluating Big6 Units of Instruction

The last project is turned in and the final presentation given. Students have even evaluated their own efforts based on the rubric or scoring guide you provided them. All is said and done. Or is it? How can we ensure that the objectives were met and the best possible instruction presented to the students?

How do teachers and library media specialist new to Big6 know if the units they design provide the most effective and efficient levels of engagement for their students? How often do those of us who have experience implementing the Big6 actually evaluate our efforts and specifically analyze each step before we present to students? We may informally evaluate our efforts after students complete the unit, but rarely do we do this before teaching. It is with this in mind that I created the Big6 Unit Evaluation Guide. Its purpose is so we leave nothing out of each step, ensuring students receive the best possible instruction we can give.

I use the guide to design effective units, as it includes the components of higher-level, integrated instruction and transferable skills. Of course, each of the items included won't be appropriate for all units. You will want to modify this guide for individual units and for your teaching style, as well as the needs of individual students and classes. However, caution is needed when omitting or changing too much—it is easy to end up with a superficial series of activities for students to engage.

The guide begins with two simple questions: Are you using the terminology of the Big6 with students, and do they know that they are engaged in a *process* as they learn the content? I find that teachers will often forget to articulate the correct labels for each step, so that in subsequent units, students are not aware that they are using the same process. You want to articulate the correct terminology so students eventually internalize the steps and understand that the process remains the same when the content changes.

Creating a good problem for Task Definition sets the stage for a successful and engaging unit. There are three main considerations here. First, is the task engaging for students, requiring higher-level thought? Do students have an opportunity to figure out what they need to and want to know before you give them a list of information to locate? And, is the task closely tied with the state or school's curriculum standards? Many times we get caught up in designing units of instruction that we love to teach, but are not included in the grade's required curriculum.

Carefully evaluating Information Seeking Strategies allows for the use of a variety of accurate and authoritative print and digital resources. Of importance here is the evaluating of sites located on the free Web. Some prefer to include Web evaluation in Step 4: Use of Information, as one must locate and begin to read the Web site in order to evaluate it for accuracy, authority, and relevance. What matters most is that *someone* evaluates sites off the free Web, whether it occurs in Information Seeking Strategies or Use of Information.

Location & Access include identifying the skills that we should teach in order for students to locate print and digital resources and access information within each. Evaluating Use of Information ensures that we teach efficient note taking skills and developmentally appropriate ways to cite sources.

The three important factors are included in Synthesis ensuring that you design a final product that allows students to add value to the information they found. We want our students to go beyond the facts and others' ideas by showing evidence of higher-level thinking. In addition, students should learn transferable skills as they show their results such as technology, composition, production, performance, and presentation skills. Last, students must give credit to their sources.

The final step of the Big6 process, Evaluation, suggests that students write about their experiences in an informal self-evaluation. Additionally, we want to include a set of predetermined criteria, probably the same one that the teacher will use for assessment such as a rubric, scoring guide, or checklist. This demystifies the expectations for the students and gives them a guideline to follow as they progress through the steps of the process. Typically this is given during Task Definition, but used as an instrument for self-evaluation.

Evaluating Big6 Units

The BIG 6

Use this guide as you are developing Big6 units for your curriculum standards or objectives. You may find that some of the items below do not meet the needs of particular objectives; however, by checking as many as possible, you will ensure that you are designing an effective and engaging unit of instruction.

___ First, are you using the terminology with the students (Task Definition, Information Seeking Strategies) as you take them through the process?

___ Do your students know that they are using a *process* to find and use information when they are engaging in Big6 units, and this process can be used any time they need information for a task or problem?

Task Definition

1.1 ___ Is the task or information problem engaging?
___ Will students want to study the content?
___ Is the task developmentally appropriate?
___ Does the task require students to think on a higher level?

1.2 ___ Do students have an opportunity to construct what they want to know, or think they need to know, about the topic *before* you tell them what they need to find out about it?
___ Are these written in question format for ease of use?
___ Is the task closely tied to the state or school's curriculum standards?
___ Does it reflect the higher-level thinking of the standards?

Information Seeking Strategies

___ Are the resources developmentally appropriate?

___ Are the resources readily available and easy to access?

___ Are the resources accessible to students who may not read on grade level? Who is able to help them?

___ Are the resources accurate, authoritative, and relevant?

___ Are students using a variety of resources?

___ Are students using a combination of digital and print resources as appropriate?

___ Which online sources (subscription-based and free Web) will your class use to complete the project?

___ How are students evaluating sites off the free Web, or are you giving them the sites they are to use?

___ Are you evaluating sites off the free Web that the students will use? (this may be performed in Big6 #4: Task Definition)

___ Which primary source materials are students using?

Location & Access

___ Are you teaching or reviewing how to locate the resources?

___ How are students accessing information within the materials? How do you know they will succeed at this?

Use of Information

4.1 ___ How do you know students will be able to access the section of the resource in which the information appears?

4.2 ___ Are you teaching or reviewing how to take notes?

___ Cite sources?

___ What type of note taking organizer are students using?

Synthesis

5.1 ___ How are students organizing information from a variety of sources?

5.2 ___ How are students showing evidence of higher-level thinking and original thought in the creation of the final product? How are they adding value to the information located?

___ Are students learning transferable skills (technology, composition, production, performance, presentation) in the creation of their final product?

___ How are students giving credit to the sources they used?

Evaluation

___ Do students have an informal written self-evaluation of their efforts?

___ Do students have a set of predetermined criteria to judge their efforts in a more formal way (such as a rubric, scoring guide, or checklist)? This is the instrument you will use to give them their grade(s). This instrument will usually be given during or soon after the Task Definition phase of the assignment.

After unit has been completed:

1. How successful was this Big6 unit? Will you teach it again?

2. How successful was the level of student engagement?

3. How effectively were the learning objectives or standards met?

4. How successful was your collaboration with the school library media specialist or classroom teacher(s) in the completion of this project?

5. What do you need to consider or change the next time you teach this unit?

Developed by Barbara A. Jansen, 2004. Big6 copyright Berkowitz and Eisenberg, 1990.

Big6™ Steps to Teacher and Librarian Collaboration

Big6™ Skill	Suggested Teacher Responsibilities	Suggested Librarian Responsibilities
Task Definition	▪ Teacher & librarian plan together to define an effective task for students ▪ Teacher is usually responsible for curriculum content ▪ Teacher usually introduces task to the class or may share this responsibility with the librarian	▪ Teacher & librarian plan together to define an effective task for students
Information Seeking Strategies	▪ Teacher & librarian plan together which sources students will likely use ▪ Teacher adds sources in which he or she is familiar	▪ Teacher & librarian plan together which sources students will likely use ▪ Librarian is responsible for identifying appropriate sources ▪ Librarian usually solicits input for sources from class and introduces new sources
Location & Access	▪ Teacher & librarian plan together the most efficient way students will locate sources ▪ Teacher will usually teach skills such as using indexes, table of contents, skimming & scanning ▪ Responsibility of teaching Internet searching may be shared	▪ Teacher & librarian plan together the most efficient way students will locate sources ▪ Librarian is usually responsible for teaching students how to access sources ▪ Librarian will usually teach students location skills related to library resources, including online subscription databases ▪ Responsibility of teaching Internet searching may be shared
Use of Information	▪ Teacher & librarian plan together effective strategies for students to acquire information, such as skimming, scanning, and note taking methods ▪ Teacher usually instructs students in note taking strategies, but responsibility may be shared ▪ Both teacher and librarian may take responsibility to assist students in their note taking	▪ Teacher & librarian plan together effective strategies for students to acquire information, such as skimming, scanning, and note taking methods ▪ Both teacher and librarian may take responsibility to assist students in their note taking
Synthesis	▪ Teacher & librarian plan together transferable and higher-level ways students can show results of information finding ▪ Teacher usually teaches skills students need to show their results, but may share responsibilities with librarian	▪ Teacher & librarian plan together transferable and higher-level ways students can show results of information finding
Evaluation	▪ Teacher & librarian plan together how students will evaluate their efforts, both process and product ▪ Teacher usually administers to students a self-evaluation instrument such as a checklist, rubric, scoring guide ▪ Teacher shares these with librarian so the process can be assessed	▪ Teacher & librarian plan together how students will evaluate their efforts, both process and product ▪ Librarian may also share in the responsibility of formally assessing students (the grading process)

*Teacher is defined as classroom teacher; campus instructional technologist; Special Education teacher; Gifted and talented teacher; special area teacher, such as art, music, or physical education; paraprofessionals responsible for instruction; or any combination of the above.

Figure 13.12: Big6 Strategies for Computer Collaboration

Big6™ Strategies for Computer Collaboration*

Big6™ Skill	Strategies for Collaboration
Task Definition	■ Group brainstorms information needed to do the task. Typically, this is written in question form. ■ Group sits around the computer. One student is designated the driver (the one who controls the mouse and inputs information) and inputs group's ideas using word processor or Inspiration. <www.inspiration.com> software. Group adds questions teacher wants included. Print enough copies for each person in group, or save to the group's folder on the server. ■ Students can take turns being the driver. ■ Best practice: have students divide the information needed (the questions) so each person has a responsibility to find some information.
Information Seeking Strategies	■ Group can use a word processor or Inspiration software to brainstorm a list of sources to help answer their questions. ■ To this, students can add sources given by their teacher and librarian. They should choose the best sources with the help of their teacher and librarian.
Location & Access	■ One student drives (responsibility can be shared). ■ Students in the group work together under the direction of the librarian and teacher to access sources on the computer (CD-ROM and Internet). ■ As one or two students in the group are using the computer, the others can be accessing books, encyclopedias, and videos in the library.
Use of Information	■ One student can use the computer while the others use the books, encyclopedias, and videos. When finished, they trade sources. ■ Each student decides what pertinent information to use to answer his or her questions. He or she will copy and paste pertinent information into word processing or Inspiration software. Or, the student should paraphrase or summarize if necessary. ■ If students in a group are finding information together, they can help each other identify pertinent information to copy and paste, or para-phrase or summarize, into the word processing or Inspiration software. ■ Information from library books, encyclopedias, and videos should be added to the group's or individual's word processing or Inspiration software.
Synthesis	■ Group works together to organize information found in sources. ■ Group compiles the notes taken to create the content for the final product . ■ If appropriate, the group uses the available computer to create the final product.
Evaluation	■ If the scoring rubric, guide, or checklist is available electronically, the group will complete it together. ■ Each student will complete an informal self-evaluation.

*Computer Collaboration is defined as a group of two or more students around one computer, as opposed to one-to-one ratio of students to computers. Many classrooms and libraries have only enough computers for students to share. This can be more effective than each student using his or her own computer in a lab, as students learn the skills of working together toward a common goal.

Big6™ in Six Minutes

Introducing the Big6 to your faculty will take longer than six minutes. However, for those faculty meetings or department meetings with full agendas, six minutes will keep even the most cynical faculty member focused. If you do not have the luxury of a day, half-day, or hour, then take what you can get! Reserve 10-15 minutes in a faculty or department meeting; the ideas below will take approximately six minutes to present, not including discussion that is sure to result.

Introducing the concept of the Big6 to faculty

Show and discuss each of the following slides, telling faculty that you will present in further detail at a department meeting, or collaborate with them, teaching their students while they learn it themselves.

Big6™ for Big Results!

The **BIG6**

Information and
Communications
Technology Skills
in the Curriculum

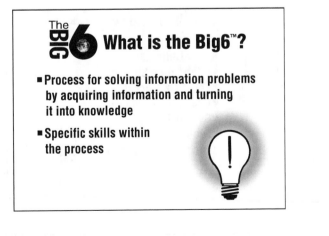

The **BIG6** **What is the Big6™?**

- Process for solving information problems by acquiring information and turning it into knowledge
- Specific skills within the process

Who can use the Big6™ skills?

Anyone who has a problem to solve or a task to complete that requires a need for information.

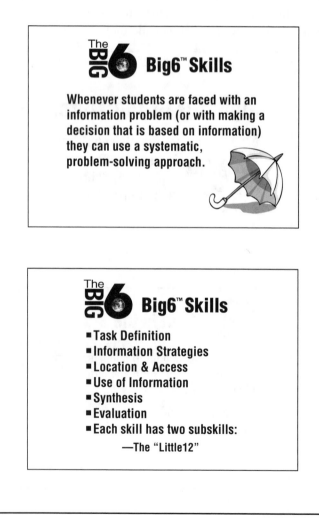

Big6™ Skills

Whenever students are faced with an information problem (or with making a decision that is based on information) they can use a systematic, problem-solving approach.

Big6™ Skills

- Task Definition
- Information Strategies
- Location & Access
- Use of Information
- Synthesis
- Evaluation
- Each skill has two subskills:
  —The "Little12"

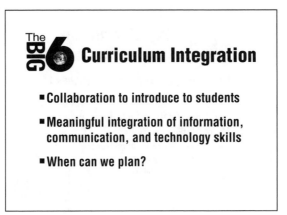

The BIG 6 Curriculum Integration

- Collaboration to introduce to students
- Meaningful integration of information, communication, and technology skills
- When can we plan?

Six Steps in Six Minutes

Present the six steps of the Big6™ to your faculty, emphasizing the efficiency with which their students will learn content skills.

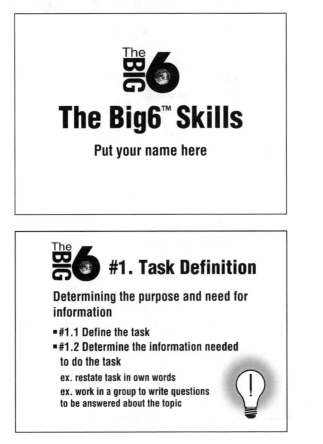

The BIG 6

The Big6™ Skills

Put your name here

The BIG 6 #1. Task Definition

Determining the purpose and need for information

- #1.1 Define the task
- #1.2 Determine the information needed to do the task

ex. restate task in own words

ex. work in a group to write questions to be answered about the topic

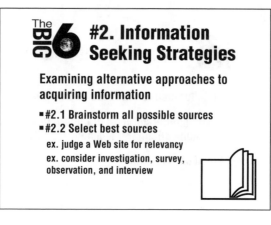

The BIG6 #2. Information Seeking Strategies

Examining alternative approaches to acquiring information

- #2.1 Brainstorm all possible sources
- #2.2 Select best sources
  - ex. judge a Web site for relevancy
  - ex. consider investigation, survey, observation, and interview

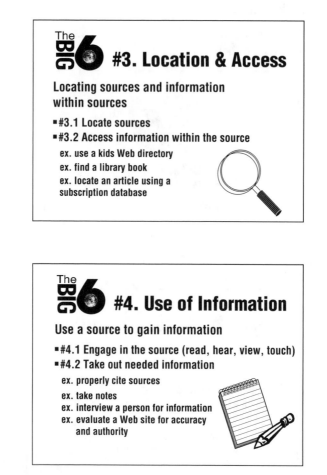

The BIG6 #3. Location & Access

Locating sources and information within sources

- #3.1 Locate sources
- #3.2 Access information within the source
  - ex. use a kids Web directory
  - ex. find a library book
  - ex. locate an article using a subscription database

The BIG6 #4. Use of Information

Use a source to gain information

- #4.1 Engage in the source (read, hear, view, touch)
- #4.2 Take out needed information
  - ex. properly cite sources
  - ex. take notes
  - ex. interview a person for information
  - ex. evaluate a Web site for accuracy and authority

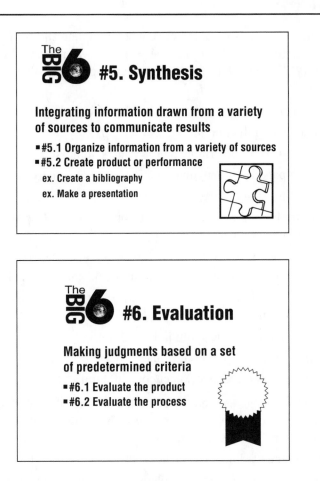

#5. Synthesis

Integrating information drawn from a variety of sources to communicate results

- #5.1 Organize information from a variety of sources
- #5.2 Create product or performance
  - ex. Create a bibliography
  - ex. Make a presentation

#6. Evaluation

Making judgments based on a set of predetermined criteria

- #6.1 Evaluate the product
- #6.2 Evaluate the process

Information and Technology Strategies in Six Minutes

Once the faculty has an understanding of the concept of the Big6 and some are even using it, you can demonstrate information skills and technology strategies, especially those that you are certain many teachers could be implementing in their courses of study. Even if some are not using the entire process, they will appreciate the brevity and usefulness of the skills, while gaining a deeper awareness of skills students should learn and apply.

Big6 4—Use of Information: Web Evaluation

Choose a Web site of questionable authority and/or accuracy. Give pairs of faculty members the Web evaluation guide you expect students to use and take them through the main points of establishing authority and accuracy. If you only have time for one, choose authority.

Encourage teachers to require students to complete and turn in Web evaluations for each site on the free Web that was not provided through the library's Web page or from a teacher. Discuss the following with the faculty:

Web site evaluation: What we want students to understand...

- Anyone can publish on the Web.
- It is often hard to determine a Web page's authorship.
- Even if a page is signed, qualifications are not usually provided.
- Sponsorship is not always indicated.
- Unlike traditional print resources, resources on the free Web rarely have editors and or fact-checkers.
- Currently, no Web standards exist to ensure accuracy. (Beck 2006)
- Considering using one of these questionable sites for establishing authority:

  <http://www.martinlutherking.org/>

  <http://www.crystalinks.com/judaism.html>

  <http://www.usahistory.com/frames.htm>

  <http://www.barefootsworld.net/constit0.html>

Demonstrate to teachers that by using the advanced search feature of Google, their students will search more efficiently. Here are the steps you may use in your demonstration:

1. Type george washington into the regular search field (How many hits?)
2. Click on Advanced search. Delete george washington.
3. With exact phrase *George Washington* (How many hits?)
4. Notice quotation marks in search bar
5. Go back to Advanced search
6. Without the word *university* (How many hits?)
7. Go back to Advanced search
8. With all of the word *president* (How many hits?)

Work cited:

Beck, Susan. "Evaluation Criteria." *The Good, the Bad, and the Ugly: Or Why It Is a Good Idea to Evaluate Web Sources.* 14 May 2006. New Mexico State University Library. 5 Sept 2006 <http://lib.nmsu.edu/instruction/evalcrit.html>.

Location and Access: Edit... Find on Web pages

Demonstrate how to use the Edit...Find feature on an Internet browser's toolbar to quickly locate words on a Web page, instead of scrolling and scanning.

Synthesis: Plagiarism

Discuss the reasons why some students plagiarize: Sometimes students do not realize that they have to give credit to a source when they summarize or paraphrase someone else's ideas. Or, they may be afraid that their own ideas are not worthy. Some students may procrastinate on an assignment and not have time to compose original ideas, being forced to cheat to get the assignment in on time. The subject matter of the assignment may be uninteresting and a student chooses to copy from someone else instead of learning it for himself. Occasionally, a student may lack integrity and behave dishonestly in various aspects of his or her life, including cheating on schoolwork. Whatever the reason, plagiarism is dishonest and must be avoided. Here are some ways teachers can help students to avoid plagiarizing:

1. Talk to your students about plagiarism and your expectations.
2. Create higher-level assignments—make it so that the students cannot just copy from books or the Internet.
3. Make reasonable timeline with check-ups.
4. Show knowledge of research paper databases—let kids know that you know. Buy one or print off a free one and analyze it with class.
5. Ensure that students know how to and when to quote, summarize, paraphrase, and cite sources.
6. Make sure students understand the concept of intellectual property and copyright laws.
7. Require early, an enhanced annotated bibliography, as appropriate.
8. Check notes periodically.
9. Require drafts and assess them.
10. Familiarize yourself with the students' writing style.
11. Have students turn in notes and graded drafts with final copy.
12. As often as possible, have students defend ideas and results.

Synthesis: Plagiarism Checker

Demonstrate to faculty how to use Google to check a string of words in a student essay or report for plagiarism from the free Web. Type at least eight consecutive words, putting quotation marks around them, into the Search field to see which Web pages were used without giving proper credit.

Use of Information: Note Taking Forms

Present the following note taking forms from Chapter Nine to teachers for their students' use in the classroom:

- Data chart
- Note taking form in Microsoft Word
- Note taking with PowerPoint

Use of Information and Synthesis: Citing Sources

Introduce an online service such as Citation Machine <http://citationmachine.net> to faculty. Fill in the fields using a good-natured faculty member's name and interest for the book or Web site title. Click "Make Citation" and listen for the sounds of awe and laughter! Show how to copy and paste to a note taking organizer or to a word processing document to make a bibliography.

Index